RICHARD WEAVER'S
LIFE STORY

RICHARD WEAVER'S
LIFE STORY

EDITED BY

REV. JAMES PATERSON, M.A., B.D.

Of White Memorial Free Church, Glasgow

"HE GAVE . . . EVANGELISTS"
(*Eph. iv. 11*)

MORGAN & SCOTT LD.
12, PATERNOSTER BUILDINGS
LONDON, E.C.

CHRISTIAN BIOGRAPHIES

In Cloth Boards. **1s. 6d.**

LIFE OF DUNCAN MATHESON.
By Rev. JOHN MACPHERSON. *With Portrait.*

LIFE OF HENRY MOORHOUSE.
By Rev. JOHN MACPHERSON. *With Portrait.*

R. C. MORGAN: HIS LIFE AND TIMES.
By his Son, GEORGE E. MORGAN, M.A. *With Introduction by Right Hon. Lord Kinnaird. Four Photogravures and Eight Half-Tones.*

MORGAN AND SCOTT LD.
LONDON.

PREFACE.

WHEN I looked through the materials entrusted to me, I was greatly delighted at the discovery that it would be possible for me to allow Weaver himself, in his own way, to tell the larger part of his life-story. I noticed, however, that if I adopted that plan, it would take me over the same ground that Mr. R. C. MORGAN, of *The Christian*, has travelled over in his "*Life of Richard Weaver.*" But I must either do that, or issue a Life that was rather a supplement to Mr. Morgan's than an attempt at a complete Life. I resolved to aim at completeness; and I therefore proceeded as if there were no account of Weaver's wonderful life already in the field. I have done this with Mr. Morgan's consent and approval.

When dealing with Weaver's account, I have kept to his words and style as rigidly as possible. Sometimes I have altered the form of the expression, but I have never allowed myself to make any alteration of the thing expressed. The division into chapters and the headings are my own.

I am largely indebted to the proprietors of *The Christian* for permission to use the notices of Weaver's missions, that are strewn in such abundance throughout the pages of their God-fearing journal; also for many valuable suggestions regarding the use of the material entrusted to me.

I must also express my great indebtedness to the family of the late evangelist, for furnishing me so liberally with the material necessary for an accurate account of their honoured relative's life, and also for aiding me in every way possible in the enquiries that I had to make. I am heartily at one with Mr. Weaver's widow in the desire expressed in one of her letters regarding this work:—"I am anxious for the account of my dear husband's life-work to be a means of great and eternal blessing to many souls."

That God will make it such is my earnest prayer.

JAMES PATERSON.

INTRODUCTION.

MANY of God's people remember the great Revival in the United States, in 1856, when a financial panic was the means of bringing thousands to prayer, and through prayer to faith in Christ. This wave of spiritual life reached Ireland and England in 1859. The years which followed were marked by a spiritual power the like of which multitudes of Christians are longing again to see.

But even earlier than 1856 a work of the same kind was in progress in the Midland Counties, of which RICHARD WEAVER, though not the originator, was the most prominent of the working-men preachers. He did not come to London until 1860. I very soon made his acquaintance; and, from that time until God called him from service on earth to rest in heaven, we were fast friends, without a break; and, when I came to know his wife, I perceived that God had given him a helpmeet for him, to whose quiet and prayerful influence much of the blessing which attended him was due.

Richard was a man of a childlike spirit. Few could so readily or so deeply touch the springs of sympathy in other souls. He knew the sorrows of the poor; the temptations and trials peculiar to the working classes; the troubles as well as the delights of little children: and his audiences responded to his touch with tears of penitence, and smiles, and songs of joy.

His perceptive faculties were very keen. Nothing escaped his notice, and his discourses were illustrated by everything he saw. He had no secrets, and the utmost confidence and sympathy were established between him and his hearers before he had got through his introductory remarks.

We know, on the Highest Authority, that a prophet is not without honour, save in his own country, and yet there may be exceptions even to this rule. Alike in his unconverted days, when his mates surnamed him "Undaunted Dick"; in the early days of his conversion, while still in the coal-pit; when called thence to be a preacher to thousands out of doors and in; and when sorely smitten by the archers and for a while "dropped," as he has said, by some who had surrounded him in his days of sunshine, he was subsequently, as well as previously to this, always respected and beloved at home. He might truly have said, "I dwell among mine own people." They knew him best, and whenever he preached they thronged to hear him.

He was a man of like passions with Elijah and ourselves, but he was true to God and true to his Gospel; and few men, if any, more simply expounded the Word as the truth is in Jesus. I have loved few men as I loved RICHARD WEAVER, and I hope soon to sing with him in the glory-land of which he often spoke— the hymn which, when I first heard him sing it, thrilled me as no other has done before or since:

> My heart is fixed, Eternal God,
>   Fixed on Thee;
> And my immortal choice is made—
>   Christ for me!
> He is my Prophet, Priest, and King,
> Who did for me salvation bring,
> And while I've breath I mean to sing
>   Christ for me!

He never attempted to fathom the mysteries of God. His gift was that of an evangelist, and most faithfully he ministered the gift imparted to him. Sin and its consequences here and its penalties hereafter; justification by grace, by blood, by faith, by works; Christ the end of the law for righteousness to every one that believeth—in a word, Jesus Christ and Him crucified: this He preached with luminous clearness, and thousands were brought into the Kingdom of God. There are probably no places where he preached where some of them may not still be found.

R. C. MORGAN.

CONTENTS.

		PAGE
I.	PERSONAL REMINISCENCES	9
II.	EARLY YEARS	29
III.	CONVERSION AND RESTORATION	45
IV.	A CHRISTIAN WORKING-MAN	62
V.	A CHRISTIAN'S SWORD EXERCISE	75
VI.	INCIDENTS IN THE WARFARE	99
VII.	THE LONDON CAMPAIGNS	116
VIII.	IN SCOTLAND	129
IX.	IN IRELAND, WALES, AND DREAMLAND	145
X.	HOLDING THE FORT AT HOLLINWOOD	155
XI.	A TRUE COMRADE	173
XII.	RE-VISITING FORMER BATTLE-FIELDS	187
XIII.	STONES FROM WEAVER'S SLING	197
XIV.	FROM THE SOLDIER'S LETTER-BAG	214
XV.	HONOURABLE DISCHARGE	224
XVI.	WREATHS FOR THE WARRIOR'S COFFIN	231

RICHARD WEAVER'S
LIFE STORY.

I.

Personal Reminiscences.

RICHARD WEAVER was nearly "made" before I knew him. At the time of my introduction to him he was sixty and five years of age. Forty years had passed since the day on which he discovered that the attempt to be a *self-made* man was sure to end in his becoming a *self-ruined* man. In order that he might become a *God-made* man, he put himself into the hands of the Maker of Israel; and for those forty years the Heavenly Potter had been working at that vessel. A few more touches, and the vessel would be finished.

It was while those finishing touches were being given that I was accorded the privilege of intimate friendship with the veteran evangelist. Knowing him only thus, I was delivered from the temptation warned against in the proverb: "Fools and bairns should never see things half made." It was far beyond that stage with Richard Weaver before Providence allowed me to make his acquaintance. The vision that I have of him is therefore more likely to be correct than it would have been had I received my first impressions of him while he was at a stage in which he could be looked upon as only half-made.

My introduction to him was brought about in the following way. In the course of visitation as minister of the English Presbyterian Church in Belgravia, London, I called one evening on a friend, who pressed me hard to go and hear Richard Weaver preach the Gospel in Pimlico Rooms. I imagined I could not spare the time. In addition, although I had no personal knowledge of the evangelist, I had somewhat of a prejudice against him. But my friend would not be put off, and at last, for the sake of peace, I consented to go.

In attending that meeting I had no other motive than that of pleasing an earthly friend. I came away from that meeting wishing I were a better man and a more faithful minister. On that evening I had irrefragable proof that God was with the aged evangelist. Without any pressing I returned on the following evening. My impression that God was co-working with the evangelist was confirmed. What I felt, heard, and saw, reminded me of the record of those who preached the Lord Jesus in Antioch: "The hand of the Lord was with them, and a great number believed and turned to the Lord."

I sought an introduction to the honoured worker. I begged him to come and preach to us in Belgrave. He consented. After he had preached, our Session appealed to him to conduct an evangelistic mission in our church. He was able to give us ten days. The more I saw of him, the higher became my esteem, and the stronger became my affection for him. In mental grit he was far above the average. He was also an orator of the first water. Indeed, he was what is called "a born genius." But though the attraction of his natural gifts was great, he had a far greater. He was of the race of whom the Prophet was speaking when he said: "Nations that knew not thee shall run unto thee, because of the Lord thy God, and for the Holy One of Israel; for He hath glorified thee."

The managers of the mission in Pimlico Rooms told me that Weaver had left the matter of remuneration entirely in their own hands. It was so in his dealings with us also. For many years he had been in such an enfeebled state of health that he was quite unable to work for more than two or three months out of the twelve. His income was, therefore, exceedingly uncertain.

From the time that he left his work in the coal-pit he looked on God as his Paymaster. In the coal-pit he was able to count on a steady £3 per week. It was not so as an evangelist. Like Paul, he was allowed to know what it was to abound; he also knew what it was to suffer want. He, too, had his wilderness temptation of hunger. On one occasion, while being used of the Holy Spirit to sway men God-ward, as few have swayed them, his food for four days was a turnip, begged from the farmer in the field. *That* did not sorely vex him; but when weeping children pleaded with him to give them breakfast first and read the Bible afterwards, and there was no breakfast to give them, then was his heart torn. Still, he retained his integrity. He looked on the suggestion to conduct no mission, save when there was a formal bargain about remuneration, as a temptation of Satan. God gave him grace to resist it to the end. He trusted God. He trusted man. Thus, his preaching of the glorious Gospel was not marred by unseemly hagglings, behind the scenes, over money. In this respect we found him *a delightful man to deal with*.

In another respect, also, he stood the testing well. He was *a delightful man to live with*. During those ten days when he preached to us in London, he was unable, on account of the distance, in his enfeebled state of health, to stay in our home. He, therefore, accepted the hospitality of a friend who lived near the church. That friend was never weary of telling me what a treasure Richard Weaver was in the home. It was with the evangelist's presence as it was with the presence of the Ark of God in the house of Obed-edom. So my friend testified. To his testimony on that point I am now able to add my own. Since coming to Glasgow we have twice had Richard Weaver's help—on each occasion for a fortnight. He stayed on these occasions in our home. It was then I was taken behind the scenes, and had revealed to me the secret of the evangelist's gracious life.

He was a great sufferer. For this discovery I was scarcely prepared. His face seemed aglow with health. He had a bright and cheery manner. In the pulpit there was such an exhibition of physical vigour, that no one who had not lived with him was prepared for the night-long sleepless suffering and the day-long prostration that combined to make his life a living martyrdom. With an energy almost superhuman, while in the pulpit, he hurled himself against the pillars of the temple of Nineteenth Century Indifference. So long as there were anxious ones to speak a word of guidance and of comfort to, his vigour held out. Then came the collapse. It was "home" to change the garments soaked with sweat until they seemed as if they had been dragged through a river. It was "home" to moan, "My head, my head," and to plead with God to give him the luxury of sleep: "If only for five minutes, Lord, do let me have it."

Again and again, while the hour of meeting drew on, the consciousness of weakness was so great, that he begged of me to free him from the address. I would, thereupon, promise to give the address myself, provided he would accompany me to the pulpit, and obviate any feeling of disappointment on the part of the audience, by telling them himself of his weakness, and speaking for not more than five minutes. And he would agree to do that; and I would conduct the earlier part of the meeting. Then he would rise with an honest intention of speaking for five minutes only: and the weakness would be forgotten; and the pleading with men to be reconciled to God would continue, till the five minutes had become fifty, and neither speaker nor audience seemed aware that the time had fled. It was on these very occasions that there seemed to be a larger measure of the power from on high. He too might have said: "When I am weak, then am I strong."

But though a great sufferer, *he had a wonderful knack of burying his sorrow.* He had nothing of cynicism or moroseness, or of morbid unhealthiness of disposition. Our children all loved him. Their eyes brightened whenever he entered the parlour. They knew that he did not despise little ones. No one in the house was more ready for fun with them than he was. In one of his poems, Whittier tells how

> The Thebaid lost its holiest *saint* and found a *man*.

We are somewhat doubtful of the saint who is not a man. And we are also somewhat doubtful of the man who is not a saint. In New Testament story the Perfect Saint is a Perfect Man. He is an absolute stranger to anything savouring of sanctimonious censoriousness. He left that to the Pharisees. Richard Weaver made Jesus his example in that respect also; and the children soon found out where the honey was. And his attention to them had its reward in their attachment to him. Knowing as I did how much suffering he was enduring, his cheery notice of the children was to me a perpetual miracle of grace. His life was fragrant with something of the fragrance that was about the life of Him of whom it is testified: "His garments smelled of aloes, and of cassia, and of myrrh."

After once getting him to lead in prayer at family worship, I never again, while he was with us, led in prayer myself. While he prayed, life was changed—what Isaiah describes as "mounting up with wings as eagles" was experienced. Nor did the blessing end there. When we rose from our knees a holier atmosphere pervaded the house. It was the consciousness of the nearness of God that did it—that morning by morning uplifting of the heart of this righteous man was the means made use of by the Shepherd of Israel to lead me for the time being to the heavenly side of life. The day began with visions of the King in his beauty, and with glimpses of the land that is usually "far, far away." I knew what it was that Bunyan clothed in picture form, when he described how it fared with the Pilgrims while they were with the shepherds on the Delectable Mountains. Even now as I write I look back on the cloud-darkened hills of memory, and see these "moments on the mount" as green and sunny patches on the shadow-covered slopes. And well I know that their brightness comes from the Sun of Righteousness.

And when the calls of duty had been attended to, and we were free to gather around the fire, we knew no greater joy than that of listening to the veteran warrior's description of some of the stirring scenes that lay so thickly bestrewn in his own past. None of his tales were second-hand. What his own hands had handled of the word of life, that he declared. His pictures were always vivid. As a word-painter he was a master-artist. He had a wonderful gift of narration. With such material to draw from, and with such a recounter, it is scarcely matter for wonder that while he talked with us our hearts burned within us.

In his fireside conversation his theme was the same that it was in his pulpit conversation. He never became tired of telling of the doings of the Lord Jesus. We listened; we pondered; then somehow there arose before our minds the inspired evangelist's description of the doings of the God-Man of Nazareth. According to the sacred writer, the crowd around HIM looked on with open-eyed amazement, and when the evening came they went to their homes to say: "We have seen strange things to-day." It was borne in on us with irresistible cogency that the name of the Christ who had been working in and through Richard Weaver, was Wonderful. Is not this the Christ of the New Testament writers?

And when we went out with the aged pilgrim, the wonders continued. We scarcely ever went into the city without being intercepted by strangers who were evidently pleased to have an opportunity of confessing that they had been "converted under Richard Weaver." I was amazed at the frequency of the recurrence of scenes that had the following outline:—

Stranger (looking hard at evangelist) asks: "Ar'n't you Richard Weaver?"

R. W. "Yes."

S. "I was converted under your preaching thirty years ago."

R. W. "Praise the Lord!"

The variant in the incident was the number of years. In some cases it was thirty-five, in some thirty, in others twenty-five, and in others ten. The number of strangers who intercepted and spoke thus to the evangelist was very large. By-and-by I began to be aware of the fact that all who spoke thus had the glow of health on the cheek and a good coat on the back. Conversion under Richard Weaver had evidently been good for the life that now is, as well as a means of removing unworthy anxiety with regard to the life that is to come. He had cast his bread on the waters, and was now reaping an abundant harvest therefrom.

Is there other field on which man may sow with the same certainty of such a blessed increase? We are not of those who think the higher critics of no use whatever. As hewers of wood and drawers of water they have their place in the sanctuary. But theirs is not a work that lies so near to the centre of things as the work of the evangelist. We have a dim suspicion that in this world of appearances the evangelist is not credited with the gift of wisdom. He may get a reputation for earnestness and for zeal; few seem to be aware of his great wisdom.

After seeing the reaping that rewarded the sower who sowed in that part of the field where evangelists sow, we are inclined to believe that there is no wise Christian who is not an evangelist. In the Christian world of our day it is the men who concern themselves with literary questions regarding the Bible that have the reputation of being men of knowledge and of penetration. The man who takes the Bible as the Sword of the Spirit, and goes forth with that heaven-forged weapon to assail the foes of his fellows, is looked on as a sort of "light-weight" in the conflict of heaven with earth. Is not such a view of evangelists a judgment according to appearances rather than a righteous judgment?

We can never forget a vision that was given us one day in Dr. Parker's City Temple. The Doctor's text was: "Things wherewith we may edify one another." In the course of his address he called attention to the wisdom of the evangelist. Making use of the devotee of the higher criticism as a foil, he startled us with the following picture: "The day of revelation has at length arrived. Higher critic and evangelist, each comes bringing his sheaves with him. We ask the higher critic to give us the result of his labours. He produces '*These generally accepted theories,*' and '*These tentative suggestions.'* We turn to the evangelist. He leads in 'The *drunkard reclaimed,* the *sin-blinded illumined,* the *weary rested,* and the *savage made a gentleman.'*" We looked at the contrast result, and felt there was a simpleton somewhere, and it was not the evangelist. Hath not God made foolish the wisdom of this world?

As I kept company with Richard Weaver and saw the outcome of evangelistic work, I too heard a voice from heaven, saying, "He that winneth souls is wise." When the Word of God is allowed to become man's critic, it makes wise the simpleton. When man becomes a critic of the Word of God, he is punished by being made a glorious fool.

As we think of these things we are reminded that it was an evangelist—John McNeill—who called our attention to the bearing of that word from the bush: "Draw not nigh hither: put off thy shoes from off thy feet." He asked what would have happened if Moses had paid no attention to the call for reverence. "Had he said to himself, 'I must, in the name of a frank and fearless criticism, go forward and take that bush up by the roots and look into the matter,' and gone forward to do so, the fire would either have withdrawn, or it would have put out his eyes." Such is McNeill's explanation of the visionless and blinded among the so-called higher critics.

And Richard Weaver was *faithful* as well as wise. He was kind-hearted as a friend. He was exceedingly willing to oblige in every way possible all who sought his company. But he would not allow his personal friendships to interfere with his work as an evangelist.

He looked on the hour of the meeting as an opportunity to be taken full advantage of. It was an opportunity that was much too precious to be treated to anything less than his best. He was therefore most conscientious in preparing for it. No matter how fascinating the after-dinner conversation; no matter how far the friend had come (and they came from as far as Dundee)—he ever kept the afternoon hours sacred for the work of preparation. He retired to his room. In meditation over his Bible and in prayer he waited upon God. Were not these hours with God the explanation of the way in which, night after night, he came forth anointed with the oil of freshness?

His preparation was not confined to the intellectual part of his being. It was a preparation of the whole man—body, soul, and spirit. In the pulpit it was Richard Weaver at his best. But it still was Richard Weaver. It was not another man that he kept to put on as a mask when he went into the sacred rostrum. A great teacher has said that so long as a speaker is conscious of a difference between the floor of the pulpit and the floor of the parlour he is not a preacher. What Richard Weaver was in the parlour *that* he dared to be in the pulpit. At a Debating Society of which I was a member, the subject one evening was: "The Pulpit and the Press." One of the members was trying to say a good word for the pulpit. Like a wise pleader he began by admitting that it laboured under certain disadvantages. Amongst these was the following (I give it in the words of the debater): "We send our young men to college to learn Divinity; and I'll be bound they do learn it. At any rate, you need a microscope if you wish to find humanity in them after they come out."

Richard Weaver was not of the class that the debater described. He for one did not allow his Divinity to swamp his humanity. From the music of his style the falsetto note was absent. In thorough-going earnestness he had few equals. His visions of life were such, that to those who were outside he cried: "*Flee from the wrath to come.*" But his vision of his Saviour was such, that to those who were within he cried: "*Serve God with mirth.*" He believed that God was his Maker. He credited God with all his gifts. He found himself the possessor of a large gift of humour: he believed that God was the Giver of that gift also. He believed in the holiness of a smile as well as in the holiness of a tear. He did not forbid the kitten to play with her tail; or the dewdrop to sparkle in the morning sunshine; or the flower to open its lips and smile on the pathway of man, the favoured child of God: and he saw no reason why he should carefully wipe away the honey from the edges of the gospel-cup of healing. He ignored that tradition of the elders.

He believed that holiness was wholeness. He knew that it was only when the right hand caused to stumble that it was to be cut off. He knew that unnatural, artificial, and manufactured solemnity had laid down far more stumbling-blocks than it had ever removed. He scorned, when standing as a witness to Him who is Truth and Reality, to give an impression of smilelessness when the smile was in his heart. He had honesty enough to believe that such inhabitants as God had placed in the heart might be permitted to show themselves at the windows. And he went "ahead on his Master's errand, turning not aside for a smile any more than he turned aside for a tear."

In the subject matter of his preaching he put *first things first*. Christened as an infant in the Church of England, confirmed also there, before Gospel light had visited his heart, it was inevitable that when the light came there should be a recoil from a ceremonialism that in his case had been devoid of meaning; and on the matter of baptism there was a recoil. And he was honest. He sought baptism at the hands of the late C. H. Spurgeon; and right joyously was it accorded. But he refused to give the ceremony anything save a secondary place. Because of this he was sometimes pestered by a class of men, who, on the matter of baptism, are arch-ritualists, and do not know it. He had his own method of dealing with such pesterers.

While he was holding a mission in Glasgow, he received an anonymous letter charging him with want of faithfulness, inasmuch as he himself was an immersed believer, and was not preaching it. Weaver read the letter to the audience and intimated that he would deal with the matter on the following evening. An eager, expectant crowd gathered for the controversy. Weaver gave out the text: "Christ sent me *not to baptize*, but to preach the Gospel"; and he preached the Gospel. Thus he bluntly refused to allow a ceremony of even Christ's appointing to become a red herring drawn across the trail of the hunter for souls. Laying wait for souls as one that had to give in an account, he shrank from "strifes of words, whereof cometh envy, strife, railings, evil surmisings." He feared controversies, that, in his experience of life, had done more for the subversion of the hearers than for their conversion.

It was quite in keeping with this settled principle that he closed his sermon on "the precious blood," with a dream which those of us who heard his telling of it can never forget. "I dreamt I was at the gate of heaven, and saw the candidates come seeking admission. The first knocked: a voice asked,

"'Who are you?'

"'A member of the Established Church.'

"'Stand back!'

"Another came and knocked.

"'Who are you?'

"'A member of the Free Church.'

"'Stand back!'

"Another came and knocked.

"'Who are you?'

"'An immersed believer.'

"'Stand back!' [In this case the 'Stand back' was given with more vehemence than on the two previous occasions.] I wondered if no one was to get in. My eye wandered away down to the earth. I saw into a workhouse. I saw an aged inmate breathe his last. He came to the gate. He knocked.

"'Who are you?'

"'A sinner trusting in the blood.'

"And the gate swung open, and a voice, in tones of heartiest welcome, said, 'Come in, thou blessed of the Lord!'"

Thus he preached. The atoning death of the Son of God had been the power of God unto salvation in his own life, and it was only what had healed himself that he recommended to others. He believed that for man there is no real rest save in Christ. He also believed that if you take away the Atonement, what is left is not the Christ of the Gospels. He could take the words of Jesus, in John xii. 32: "I, if I be lifted up from the earth, will draw all men unto Me"—and explain them in the same way in which John explained them. He was not under the necessity (as some others) of explaining away some of the words of Jesus. Nor was he under the necessity of "talking down" to such a Spirit-filled Apostle as Paul.

Paul's explanation of the death of Christ sufficed for him. It was the explanation that accorded with the facts of his own life. He knew that *sin* is an offence against God. With him, as with Moses, duty to God was the first table of the law. He knew that the wages of sin is death. He was unable to think of God as a Being of such flabby benevolence that He can be sinned against with impunity. He knew that God is a Father, ready to forgive the returning prodigal. He was not forgetful of the parable of the Prodigal Son. But he knew that Christ also made use of parables in which God is represented as a King. As a King, He has to deal with some who are servants, and also with some who are enemies. As a King, He has to care for the interests of his Kingdom. And amongst these interests is the vindication of his own law. "Forgiveness without vindication of the law is no mercy." So thought Richard Weaver. Hence his conception of the Gospel was a conception that found correct expression in the words of the New Testament.

He could allow all the words of the New Testament to stand the full strain of their legitimate meaning. He was under no temptation to handle the Word of God deceitfully. For him Calvary was a new Sinai. There the holiness of God was proclaimed with an emphasis far exceeding the emphasis of its proclamation from the old Sinai. Sin was so terrible that when the Son of God became the Sin-bearer God forsook Him. Christ's one comfort in his life of sorrow had been his consciousness that He was not alone, for the Father was with Him. And now, when his need of the Father was greatest, the Father was under the necessity of hiding his face. What agony for the Son! Still more terrible must have been the agony of the Father! What father is there who does not run to his child at its cry of pain? Shall God, the Creator of the earthly father, not have that feeling also? What explanation can be given of this unspeakable suffering on the part of the Divine Son, and this still more unspeakable suffering on the part of the Divine Father, other than the explanation given in the New Testament, "He bare our sins in his own body on the tree"?

> The Holy One did hide his face;
>   O Christ, 'twas hid from Thee!
> Dumb darkness wrapped Thy soul a space,
>   The darkness due to me.

It was this "old, old story," which had been the power of God unto salvation to Richard Weaver, that he proclaimed to others. To the man whose conscience has been atrophied by the theory of Evolution it was a gospel that was hid. To the man whose conscience was still alive it was "glad tidings of great joy." If a man can believe that "sin is only good in the making," he has no need of the Cross of Calvary. If he finds himself compelled to believe that sin is sin, black and hateful, and as sin deserving of the wrath of God, he will find rest nowhere else than at the foot of the Cross. It was men of the latter class to whom Weaver was helpful. Looking from the pulpit on a Weaver audience, I was struck with two things: (1) it was an audience composed largely of men; (2) speaking generally, the men were men whose faces were battlefields. They were capable of the feeling that prompts the question: "What must we do to be saved?" To them *justification* was a prize—to be sought above all other prizes; not a legal figment to be laughed at as a delusion that had had its day and had passed away. To them the preacher of the atoning blood was a messenger of peace. And such was Weaver.

But he was careful to proclaim the *regenerating* as well as the justifying power of the "precious blood." With him conversion was not a change of doctrinal belief merely; it was a change of heart as well. We once heard him read the fourth chapter of the first epistle of John. When he had read these words of the twentieth verse, "If a man say, I love God, and hateth his brother, he is a liar," he paused. Then with something of awfulness of emphasis he said, "And all liars of this class, as of every other class, shall have their part in the lake that burneth with fire and brimstone." To him the regenerated heart was a loving heart. He believed that God withheld his pardon from those who refused to accept, along with the gift of forgiveness, the gift of a forgiving spirit. He who thought himself saved, and yet consciously indulged in an unforgiving spirit, deceived himself. But God is not mocked. Whatsoever a man soweth that he also reaps. If he sows an unforgiving life, he reaps an unforgiven life. And God's means of implanting that forgiving, loving heart is the vision of Calvary. If God *so* love us, as to have given his Son to die for us, we ought also to love one another. Thus was Weaver a preacher both of peace and of life. 'Tis thus in the Gospels.

"Where," said the Grecians, "shall we find rest? We have tried philosophy in vain. We have tried Judaism also in vain; we are not yet at rest." And Philip told Andrew, and together they tell Jesus; and for answer Jesus pointed forward to Calvary. The rest-seekers would not find what they sought till they trod that holy hill. "How," said Nicodemus, "can a new nature be given me?" and Jesus pointed him to Calvary. There he would see the love of God. There he would with open face behold as in a glass the glory of the Lord, and the vision would regenerate his life. "The blood," said Weaver, "is precious because it regenerates as well as justifies. You get both justification and regeneration at Calvary's cross." Such was Weaver's preaching: thoroughly Scriptural. He did not separate the doctrinal from the ethical. He found these joined together by the God of the Bible; and what God had joined together he did not put asunder. Perhaps that is the reason why those who were converted under his preaching were generally found to be what the Salvationist would call "properly saved."

Familiar as I was with his preaching, and also with the gracious and consistent life that lay behind his preaching, I was quite prepared for the discovery that God had given him his own sons and daughters. Grace swept into that family circle with such effect, that for years before Weaver fell asleep he had the joy of seeing every one of his sons and daughters walking in the truth. Is not this of itself one of the most emphatic of signs that God was with him?

Such is the *vision* God gave me of Richard Weaver. To see him as I saw him was to esteem and love him. And I did esteem him with a great esteem, and love him with a sincere affection. That is probably the reason why he told his sons to ask me to write the story of his life. The invitation to do so finds me at its mercy. While he was with us, it was ever a great joy to me to drop into the seat in the corner of the pulpit and see Weaver step forth into the centre and do the preaching. I had far more confidence in his preaching than I had in my own. I am glad that relationship is still possible. As far back as I can remember we used to sing that hymn from his book—

> In the Christian's home in glory
>   There remains a land of rest,
> Where the Saviour's gone before me
>   To fulfil my soul's request.
> He is fitting up my mansion,
>   Which eternally shall stand:
> And my stay shall not be transient
>   In that holy, happy land.
>   On the other side of Jordan,
>   In the sweet fields of Eden,
>   Where the tree of life is blooming,
>   There is rest for you.
>   There is rest for the weary,
>   There is rest for you.

He has entered into that rest; nor would I call him from it. The comrade who bore the full brunt of the battle on many a well-fought field will never again accompany me to an earthly pulpit. But in this telling of the story of his life he will take the centre for me once again. By request, he sometimes told the story while he was with us. The story was taken down as he told it. The manuscript has been put into my hands. With unfeigned delight I, as of yore, take the seat in the corner of the pulpit, and allow Richard Weaver to step forth into the centre and speak for himself.

II.

Early Years.

WHEN a man has to tell of the travels of his own life, he has often to use that little word, "I." It is an unpleasant word to both speaker and hearer. I have therefore to ask you to bear with me patiently, and to pray for me. I have no wish to exalt myself. I have nothing to boast of. My only desire is to exalt Him who revealed Himself to Moses as the great and only "I AM." In consenting to tell the story of his grace to myself—one of the chief of sinners—I am moved by the hope that others who feel themselves sinners will be led to say: "If God's love and grace availed for Richard Weaver, then none need despair."

I was born in the little mining village of Asterley, in Shropshire. My father's name was George Weaver; he was a farm labourer. My mother's name was Mary They lived in a thatched cottage. They had four sons: John, the eldest; then George; then Thomas; and lastly, myself. I was born on the 25th of June, 1827. I don't know that my father's wage, from year's end to year's end, ever averaged more than ten shillings per week. There were not many dainties to be had out of that. Nowadays our children must pick and choose in their eating. You often hear some such speech as: "I can't eat that—it's fat!" When I was a boy it would have done me good to have seen either lean or fat: we were thankful to sit down to a red herring and potatoes. Sometimes my mother would buy that "choice joint, sheep's head and pluck," and right glad was I when she could give me a "sinker." But perhaps you don't know what a sinker is. Well, I'll tell you. If you put liver and lights into water, the liver sinks and the lights float: that is why the liver is called a "sinker."

But with all this absence of dainties we were happy. We would, however, have been happier far if the Lord had reigned in my father's heart. My mother had not obeyed the command, "Be not unequally yoked." I am sorry to say I was the son of a drunken father. I could tell some sad tales of sorrow that I witnessed when quite a child. Many a time have I clung to my mother, and cried to my drunken father: "Don't kill my mother!" I can remember my mother, with her arms around Thomas and myself, pleading in prayer, and my father standing over her with an axe uplifted, and swearing that he would cleave her in two if she did not give over praying. I can see her face now, tears rolling down her cheeks, as, looking at the axe, she tightened her grip on us and said to my father, "Ah! George, you cannot let it fall without God permits."

Some may jeer at prayer and say, "There is nothing in it." My own experience teaches me differently. My mother was delivered by the Stronger than the strong man. But she had her sufferings. Many times has that mother, on cold winter nights, been turned out of bed and compelled to fly out of the house with her children, and seek the shelter of the pigstye, thankful to creep in and secure the warm place in which the pig had lain as a couch for the night. Often, too, have I stood between my father and mother and caught the blow intended for my mother, and been felled thereby to the ground. But these, as you will hear by-and-by, became part of the "old things" that passed away. Prayer, through faith in Christ, at last prevailed.

I had not what we call the chances in life that children have now. At that time there was no Lord Shaftesbury pleading for shorter hours: no Macdonald or Burt had as yet arisen to plead for colliers and their children. There were no School Boards to care for the education of the young. I might say that no man cared for either our souls or our bodies.

The collier's child had to go to the pit when very young. I began when I had just turned seven. I was up in the morning at half-past four, and off to the pit. In the winter months I saw the daylight only on the Sunday. I praise God for better days for colliers. They have shorter hours now, and more time to prepare for the Sabbath. It grieves me to see the poor use that so many make of this greater leisure. I was a child, not eight years old, when I used to be raised out of bed on the dark mornings, weeping. My poor mother would go along the lane with me to the pit, encouraging me as we went.

The seam of coal that I began to work on was only thirteen inches thick. I had a piece of rope, called a girdle, put round my waist. This girdle had a chain attached to it. The other end of the chain was hooked on to a sleigh, laden with coal, and I had to crawl on my hands and knees and draw the sleigh along. The roof was not high enough to prevent my back hitting against it, nor was I able to keep my sides clear of the brushing. My back and sides were often so sore that I could scarcely hold up, but we were obliged to keep at it till it was time to go home. Then my mother used to wash me with salt and water. Only those who have gone through them can conceive the hardships of collier boys of that time. We could not be sold; but otherwise we were not better off than slaves. Down in the coal-pit from five in the morning till nine (and often till ten) at night, ours was a life of dreadful suffering.

While that is so however, I am compelled, in looking back on those days, to acknowledge that a protecting Providence was watching over me. I had many narrow escapes from death. Once I fell into a pool of water, and being unable to swim, I sank twice before I was got hold of by one of my uncles, who had seen my danger and jumped in to save me. My mother did not forget to thank God for my preservation.

At another time I fell down the pit shaft, and, as I fell, caught hold of the rails that run along the door on which the wagons are let down. There I hung, over the pit's mouth. Below me was a depth of one hundred and fifty yards. A man got into the tub, and was let down, and rescued me from death. But the Lord was in it all.

At another time a man was killed at my side. He was a Mormon, and was telling me that he was going to Salt Lake City, and that he would never die; but even while he was speaking, a stone fell out of the roof and killed him in a moment. One of my feet was caught fast underneath the stone. I have been in no fewer than six explosions. In some of these many of my fellow-workmen were burnt to death. I cannot but acknowledge the protecting care that up till now has preserved me from death.

I have, however, to confess that as I grew up I wandered away from my mother's God. She did her utmost to guide my feet into the way of peace. I can well remember the first hymn she taught me, and how she took me into a neighbour's house and put me on a chair and told me to say my hymn. It began thus:

> Happy the child whose youngest years
> Receive instruction well;
> Who hates the sinner's path, and fears
> The road that leads to hell.

How she kissed me, and thanked God, and said she believed I would be a comfort to her! Little did she think she would have to weep and pray for long and weary years before she would see what she desired.

When I went to the coal-pit and got mixed up with boys who cursed and swore and told lies, I became like them. At first I shuddered at the things they did; but by degrees that wore off. Thus one defence of the soul was broken down. By-and-by I began to think the other boys got on better than I did, simply because they cursed and swore so much; and thus was a breach made in a second defence of the soul. I remember the first time I uttered an oath. How often I wish I had not done it! When I went home at night and was going to bed, my mother saw that something was the matter with me, as I got into bed without praying. She only thought I was ill, and she said to me:

"I can see, my dear child, that you are ill to-night; so I will pray for you."

With what fervour did that mother plead with the Lord to bless her boy!

But, alas! that oath was only the beginning of sin. It was like the letting-out of water. I went on, adding one sin to another. Still the mother prayed for her erring child, and to prayer she added personal entreaty. I remember that I used to leave my work, and go into the fields; and she has followed me there for hours, entreating me, with tears, to be a good boy. It was all to no purpose. My heart was steeled against her counsel.

My poor mother! She *had* her troubles. Her husband was a drunkard, and some of her sons were beginning to walk in their father's footsteps. But the Lord did not leave her entirely without comfort. My eldest brother, John, was always kind to her. About this time he crowned his kindness by joining my mother in prayer, and going with her to the house of God.

She was a strong churchwoman, and went to the Established Church. To her there was no place of worship like the parish church. She used to take me regularly to it while I was still young and under her control. I remember, however, that I generally felt glad when the minister pronounced the benediction. I had no interest in the service, and yet I must needs be confirmed. I had been christened as an infant. Godfathers had given several solemn promises for me. They kept none of their promises. Nor did the utter neglect of their promises seem to cost them one pang of conscience, or in the least detract from their reputation. Now, I was to make the same kind of promises in my own name. I was "confirmed," along with another boy, at Westbury. Whether the bishop's hands, laid on his head, did much for the other boy, I am not to say. In my own case, it had exceedingly little effect. The moment I got outside the church, I and another youth had a fight. So was it with me immediately after my confirmation, and as I grew in years I increased in sin. My confirmation was only a confirming in sin.

About this time my brother took me away from the coal-pit and sent me to school. Instead of going to school I played truant, and spent the school-money he had given me. For this my father made me pull off my coat, and he beat me on my bare back with a rope, without mercy. But ropes' ends failed to cause my stubborn will to yield.

When I was thirteen years of age my brother John got married. On the occasion of his marriage, drink had, of course, a prominent place. Indeed, the ceremony would not have been considered complete without it. Up till that time drink had been to me like wormwood or rue tea. I had already acquired the accomplishments of dancing and boxing, and now I was to learn drinking also. They gave me one glass, and that one glass made me drunk—yes, drunk—and I was put to bed drunk at thirteen! Thus I had got fairly launched on the stream of sin. After this my mother's voice had no power to stay me. Wicked youths were my companions; drinking and fighting were my delights. And old men encouraged me in sin. Even my godfathers themselves were amongst those who incited me to fight. In these circumstances it is scarcely to be wondered at that my progress in sin was exceedingly rapid.

When but a youth of fifteen I had a dog that was famous for running and hunting. Becoming acquainted with two brothers who were great poachers, I used to go out with them, taking my dog with me, at night. After they had set their snares and nets, I used to let the dog go to drive the game into the nets. One night when I was out with them a gamekeeper accosted us. One of the brothers carried the barrel of a gun in one of his pockets and the stock in another. Putting barrel and stock together, he pointed the gun at the gamekeeper and put his finger on the trigger. The other brother knocked the barrel up, and the shot went over the gamekeeper's head. The poor man pleaded for his life, and on his promising not to inform on us, he was allowed to go. Thus my course of life was adding sorrow to sorrow to my praying mother, and provocation to provocation to my long-suffering God.

One night, when I was between seventeen and eighteen, as I was drinking with some of my mates, a man, who stood nearly six feet in height, began challenging any one in the room to fight with him. No one accepted the challenge. At last the pride of my heart arose, and I said to him, "I'll fight thee."

They said he would kill me. I replied that I could die but once. When we stripped, some one cried out: "David and Goliath." In the fight he knocked me down thirty-two times. My brother Thomas kept carrying water in his boot and throwing it over me to keep the swelling down. At last I crushed one of my opponent's eyes. Of course, after that, the fight was in my own hands, and he gave in and acknowledged that he was beaten. I thought I was a great man when they thereupon christened me, "UNDAUNTED DICK"; but I still carry the marks of that battle, and feel the effects of it, and shall feel them to my dying day. When I was at Dr. Barnardo's Homes I met a doctor whom I told about the pain I suffer. He asked me if ever I had had serious blows on the head. He said he could account for the pain in no other way. I told him of that fight. He at once told me that the pain I suffer is the outcome of that evening of sin. So true is it, that, "Whatsoever a man soweth that shall he also reap."

And yet God has granted to me a gracious forgiveness of that hour of sin. Years after that fight I was preaching in a little Primitive chapel; the place was crowded. A tall man, with grey head, and blind of one eye, sat on the pulpit steps. I saw the tears running down his cheeks. When I came down from the pulpit, he took me by the hand, and pointing to his sightless eye, said:

"Do you see that? Do you know me?"

I had forgotten him; but he went on to say:

"You did that; but, praise God, I can now see Jesus as my Saviour, and I am on the way to heaven with thee, Richard!"

We praised God together.

At another time, my poor old mother got me a new suit of clothes. When she saw me with them on, one Sunday morning, I suppose she thought me the finest looking young man in the village. Off I went with my godfather and others of my companions for a "spree." We went to an old village inn, called "The Red Lion." By-and-by the lion began to roar. One of the men drinking there wanted to fight some one. I must needs take up the challenge. Tables and benches were removed; the room cleared, and the door locked. No one could come in or go out. We stripped, and I pulled off my shoes to avoid slipping. We fought for upwards of an hour. I again was proclaimed the victor, but I was fearfully disfigured. I was carried the two miles that lay between the scene of the fight and my home. When we arrived we found that my father and mother had gone to rest. We knocked; a voice at once replied:

"I am coming, my child!"

When the door was opened, what a sight met my mother's gaze! My face was covered with blood; one eye was closed, and the other nearly so; my hands were swollen, my trousers in tatters and stained with blood. Oh, the tears of that mother as she washed the wounded body of her son!

Then happened what I can never forgive myself for. She prayed to God to save her lad. While she prayed I cursed and swore that I would murder her if she did not leave off. I went to bed: my mother knelt by my bedside and continued to pray. In a rage I sprang out of bed, and grasping her grey hair, shook her while she was still on her knees. She took hold of my hand, and said:

"Ah, Lord, this *is* hard work; but bless my boy, and save him!"

Her faith was sorely tried; but God has heard that prayer.

Having begun to walk in the counsel of the ungodly, I went on adding sin to sin. I began to frequent ball-rooms and dancing saloons, and often spent a whole week (sometimes even a fortnight) in drunken revelry. When my poor mother came to the public-house seeking for her lad, the publican would hide me, and say I was not there. I could sing and dance and keep the company alive, and that sort of thing is what the landlords like. Men that were husbands and fathers led me on. At last, matters came to such a pass that my master met me one day and said:

"Dick, my gamekeeper says he thinks he saw you with some men that threatened to shoot him: now, if I find you are amongst poachers, and if you are caught, I will send you where you will not get away from for a week or two."

It helped to make me tired of home. I was tired of my mother's prayers and conversation. Yet many times the Spirit of God strove with me, and caused me to go on my knees and pray for mercy. Like the morning cloud and early dew, these seasons passed away. I had not seen myself as I was, nor realized my lost and ruined condition. I loved sin and wickedness, and was not willing to give up all for Christ. All love for my mother left me. One night I struck her to the ground. Young men and women, let me entreat you, yea, let me beseech you to be kind to your parents; and if you have praying parents, prize them. Never mind the scoffs and sneers that such an attitude to your parents may draw on you. Take advice from one who has shed many and bitter tears when he has thought on his unkindness to his mother.

At this time I was in the Oddfellows' Club, and I made it up with another member of that club to leave home. Our parents gave us money to pay the subscription to the club; but instead of doing so we each put on two shirts, and set off. My three brothers were at that time living at a place called Bradley Green, in Staffordshire, and we started for that place. A man who worked with us accompanied us for four miles, trying to persuade us to return. Then he left us, in tears. We walked on until it was far into the night. At last we reached the town of Tunstall, and put up at "The Hanging Gate." Footsore and weary we again went on, until we arrived at the colliery where my brothers were working. We stayed in the cabin on the pit bank till they came up the shaft. They gave me a good scolding for leaving my home and my parents; but my brother John allowed me to live with him.

Having thus got away from home and free from all restraint, I soon began to be the boon companion of drunkards and gamblers. I took the keenest pleasure in fighting; it was my greatest joy to batter and deface the image of God. I was now one of the most active servants of the devil. The following incident will show the depths of wickedness into which I had descended. One day, when I was drinking with some of my companions, a poor fallen woman did something that vexed me. I took hold of a rope and, twisting it round her neck, flung the other end over a hook in the beam, and pulled her up. She struggled for life. One of my companions took out his knife and cut her down. Is it not a mercy I'm out of hell? Praise be to God for his sovereign grace!

"O'er ruin's brink I almost fell;" but my mother

kept on pleading for me at the throne of grace. She also used to write letters, which were always left for me at one of the inns in Congleton. I was not able to read them, but I used to get one of my companions to read them to me. My mother generally closed her letters with the words, "I will never give thee up." One day the reader of the letter asked me what she meant by that.

"Why, that she will never give up praying for me," was my reply. "Burn it, Tom," I said.

"Nay," he said, "it will never do to burn thy praying mother's letter."

And the tears rolled down his cheeks as he added:

"I wish I had a praying mother. I wish my mother were alive, Dick. Her last words to me when she was dying were: 'Thomas, my son, will you meet me in heaven?' And by God's help I will. Give me thy mother's letter."

There and then he bade me good-night, and left me. I never saw him again; but after I was brought to Christ I received a letter from his brother-in-law, enclosing my mother's letter, and also stating that it was the turning point in his life, and that he had died in peace and joy in the Holy Ghost.

Come with me now, while I picture to you a young man with bloodshot eyes, and burning brow, and bloated cheeks; with dry and parched lips; with troubled heart and downcast look, just risen from his bed after frightful dreams of the infernal pit, and devils saying to him:

"Thou art too bad to live; thy home deserted;

thy character blasted; thy constitution broken; and every one frowning on thee: put an end to thy life!"

Such are my recollections of myself at the age of twenty-four. Driven and tossed by the waves of these fierce temptations; smarting under the sting of an accusing conscience; ashamed of being seen in the streets with my drunkard's heavy head; with pockets empty—I resolved to take my own life. Follow me upstairs and see me there, on my knees but not to pray. Look at the young man: untying his neckerchief; taking a razor from his box; he cannot write, but with chalk he makes strokes on the floor that he hopes will be understood by his landlady; he kneels over a basin:—yea! over the mouth of the pit itself! Ah! my soul shudders at the remembrance of that awful moment. But I also thank God for his saving grace; for as I knelt I heard a voice, saying:

"Remember that old woman in Shropshire that cried in her prayers, 'Lord, save my lad.'"

I paused. I shook. I trembled. I wept, and I cried: "What will she say when she hears that I have sent my soul into eternity before its time?"

No one can imagine the struggle of my mind; but I believe the Lord was there. He had my mother's prayers before Him, and it was with me as with Job of old: the Lord would not let Satan take my life. Casting the razor away, I ran downstairs and said to my landlady:

"I have been tempted to cut my throat. You will find the razor on the floor upstairs." She threw up her hands in fear, and cried:

"Anything but that! The Lord have mercy on thee,

Dick!" I began to wring my hands, and curse the day that I was born; but she said: "The Lord bless thee, lad! Thank God, thee'st yet alive! There's hope for thee yet."

How can I describe the horrors that I went through at the time! I think sometimes that hell itself cannot be worse than the torments I suffered.

But the interposition of God's restraining mercy had made no lasting impression on me. On I went as before. Satan had not a more active servant in all his ranks than Richard Weaver. I went, as the saying is, "The whole hog for hell."

About this time I heard that my brother George was converted. He had been a rough character; but my mother had been praying for him also, and the Lord had answered her prayers for him. My eldest brother had years before been brought to a knowledge of Christ, so that two of my brothers were now on the Lord's side; but that had no effect on me. Fighting was my delight, and I can assure you I was never short of a job. Many a night I lay in bed so badly punished as not to be able to turn over. "The way of transgressors is hard." The Devil pays poor wages.

Walking out one day, shortly after George's conversion, I met a man who worked at the same colliery with him, and asked how my brother was. The man told me he was well. He also told me that a man had greatly insulted him by spitting in his face. My brother had to measure the work and book time, and it was over something in connection with these things that the dispute had arisen. I asked my friend what my brother did when the other spat in his face.

"What Christ did," was the answer. "George only said: 'Father, forgive him, for he knows not what he does.'"

I said: "Tell my brother he can forgive him; but tell that man I will come and pay him."

A week or two after this, I went over to Biddulph, during the "wakes," to pay the man that spat in my brother's face. I entered a public-house, and was made heartily welcome by my old companions in drink.

"Undaunted," says one, " drink with me."

"Undaunted," says another, "I'm glad to see thee."

I soon spied the man I wanted to pay. I got up and said I would fight the best man there. He jumped up and said:

"I suppose you mean me."

"Yes," I said, "you are just the man I have come to see."

We went outside and fought on the hard road. The master of the colliery and his brother (who was a constable) came up with a pair of handcuffs.

"Come, Harry," said he, "let us put them on him."

"Stand back, master," I said, "I have already beaten four men, and now I will beat you."

I made for him. He ran off, calling out, "Come away; he has gone mad." Yes, I was mad—mad with drink and sin. In after years I went to preach at that place. That master sent for me to call and see him. He opened the door himself. He put out his hand. His eyes filled with tears as he said, "What hath God wrought!"

III.

Conversion and Restoration.

IN the year 1852 I again went to live with my brother George. He was now a preacher on the Primitive Methodist plan. My mother was still pleading with the Lord for her prodigal son, Richard. But I was still the same. I was under an engagement to fight a man on Saturday, May 21st. On the Wednesday night preceding the Saturday on which the fight was to come off, I lay on my bed planning and scheming how to beat my opponent.

It is easy to win in your imagination; and I had planned it all out in such a way in my own mind that I already felt certain of victory. But there was to be another fight before mine should take place. The lion of the tribe of Judah and the roaring lion of hell were already in the ring. My brother had been to a cottage meeting that Wednesday night; and as I lay there thinking, I heard him come in and go into the kitchen His wife asked:

"What was the text, George?"

He made answer, "What then shall I do?"

She said, "Be off with thee; that's no text."

"I tell thee it is," said he.

"And who was the preacher?" asked his wife.

"Thomas Booth."

"Yes," said she, "it's like old Tommy."

Now as I lay there hearing their talk I thought to myself, What a funny text! I could not read at that time; but I pondered the matter over in my own mind in this way. "What then shall I do?"—there must be something more than that. Then I thought, What shall I do when God rises up in judgment against me? I turned over in my bed and heaved a deep sigh. Ah! I thought, I shall be damned. The Spirit of God carried that text into my heart, and fixed it there like a nail in a sure place. Oh, that night! Shall I ever forget it? I could not sleep; I could not pray. A conflict was raging between the powers of heaven and the powers of hell, and my heart was at once the battle-ground and the prize. The devil kept reminding me of the coming fight, and kept saying, "If you get converted now, they will think you are afraid of fighting that man." There he had me. I think sometimes that no one ever went through such a conflict as I did. I felt as if I already realized what it is to be damned.

That night passed away, and morning came. When it was time to get up and go to work, my brother called me. I said I was not going. He asked me what was the matter. I said I had a pain in my back. How readily that lie was given me! I had no pain whatever in my back; the pain was in my heart. I was afraid to go to the coal-pit, lest I should be killed, and go straight to hell. I was under the awful brow of Mount Sinai; the thunders crashing, and the lightnings of God's wrath flashing around me. All that day I was wretched. I could not eat. I could do nothing. When my brother came home at night, his wife said to him:

"I am sure our Dick is ill. He has not touched food to-day."

My brother came to me, and asked if he should fetch the doctor.

"No," I said; "I don't want *him*."

I wanted forgiveness of sin, and I knew the Lord alone could give me that. But there was that *if* in my way—"*If* you get saved they will say you were afraid to fight."

Again I lay on my bed on the Thursday night, groaning and tossing. I durst not offer to look to God, nor pray. Again the battle was being waged, and it seemed as if all heaven and hell were watching to see which side would gain the victory. On Friday morning I said to myself, "I'll go to Congleton and get drunk, and drive the thought away." Away I went those four miles to Congleton, and spent seven shillings in rum. I had a sparring match with a noted pugilist as well. When I left to go home along the lonely lane, in the dark, what a state I was in! No one but the Lord knows what I went through during that four miles' walk. Every step I took the earth seemed opening to swallow me up. I fell on my knees, and asked God to spare me till the morning; promising if He did spare me to go and pray in the field I was to fight in. Before I reached home I was as sober as I am now.

About two o'clock on Saturday morning I went into the field, as I had promised, and there, in a sand-hole, I fell on my knees. My mother's prayers were nearing their answer. I did not know what to say. No eye but God's saw me. There was a struggle between life and death. There I knelt, trembling from head to foot.

D

At last I said, "Now, Lord Jesus, I am on my knees; and I will shut my eyes, and will not open them again till Thou, for thine own Name's sake, hast pardoned my sins."

My poor old mother was nearly a hundred miles away. The devil whispered, "You don't know whether you are elected or not." Still I remained on my knees, and as I, with closed eyes, waited on the Lord, I thought I heard my mother's voice, saying: "My dear boy, 'God so loved the world that He gave his only-begotten Son, that whosoever believeth in Him should not perish, but have everlasting life.'" Ah! I thought, if He loved the world, He loved me—poor me; and, as a proof of his love, He gave his only-begotten Son as a gift to me. Now, I did not understand what "faith" or "believing" meant; but I had heard that it was taking God at his word. I took God at his word. I accepted his gift. I believed God's love, and found that that "whosoever" included me also. There and then joy and peace came into my heart.

> Soon as my all I ventured
> On the atoning blood,
> The Holy Spirit entered,
> And I was born of God.

Over that sand-hole there was rejoicing in heaven. The Shepherd had found his lost sheep, and had laid it on his shoulders rejoicing, and the return journey to the home-fold was begun.

That was the turning point in my life. I went to that sand-hole, condemned, guilty: I returned to the house justified by faith. A moment before, a brand for the burning; now a tree of righteousness, the planting of the Lord, that He might be glorified.

The happiness I then enjoyed I cannot describe. My peace flowed as a river. With what joy did I tell the good news! Like the woman of Samaria, I said: "Come, see the Christ!" but wasn't I astonished at the reception given to my testimony! I went straight to my sister-in-law, and told her that Christ had saved me. She said:

"I don't believe it; I must see how you live before I believe it."

When my brother came home, I told him what great things God had done for my soul. He looked rather doubtful, and said:

"I hope it's true; we shall see in time."

You see, I got but little encouragement from my earthly friends; but my joy was in the Lord, and my boast was in the God of my salvation.

Oh, the happiness of my soul! I thought even the trees looked different; and the birds—these warbling songsters—seemed to be helping me to praise our God. With what delight did I get a Christian man to write my mother and tell her that her prayers were answered. *She* believed the good news. I found out afterwards that when she received the letter she took it from house to house telling the neighbours what the Lord had done for her prodigal son; she could not sleep at night for weeping, and praising God for answering her prayers. She kept saying: "I will never doubt the Lord again."

Now I began to think what I had to face. I counted the cost, and went to the Lord for strength to take my stand and confess Christ.

On the Sabbath immediately following the Saturday

of my conversion, my brother George was "planned" to preach and hold a love-feast at a chapel in the neighbourhood. I thought I would go with him, and tell them there what the Lord had done for my soul. When I arrived I found myself unable to say a word.

I came back to Bradley Green, and felt I must speak there. I went round and invited some of my old companions to go to chapel with me. Seven of them went. When the minister invited any who wished to be saved to come forward, I said to one who sat by me:

"Go up and be saved."

He said: "I will go if thou wilt."

I spoke to another, and got the same answer. I said: "Well, come along." They all followed me, and all professed to find the Saviour. That was a grand night. I remember I made my chamber ring with praise to God, till my brother and his wife begged me to go to sleep and let them get a little rest.

When morning came, I went to my work at the pit, and found that it had spread far and wide that "Undaunted Dick" had got saved. Very few believed it. Others mocked and said:

"We shall see at the Club-Feast."

Others said they would give me three weeks. As I went towards the cabin that morning, I breathed the prayer, "Lord, help me to confess Thee." When I got inside, I noticed they were looking at each other and at me. There were the wink and the nod which said: "Now we've got him."

"Well, Undaunted," asked one, "is it true thee'st got converted?"

"Oi," said I. (I had not learned to say "yes" then.)

"Is it a fact?" asked another.

"Oi," I said again.

A large number of them asked similar questions, and I gave to all the same answer.

I looked at them; there were thirty-two of them.

"Now, chaps," I said, "the Lord has pardoned my sins, and I am on my way to heaven; what can you make of it?" There was silence for a time, and then one said:

"I wish I was saved."

Another said: "I wish the Lord had pardoned my sins."

They were all of one mind; and in after years the most of them were led to Christ. I like to see young converts, as soon as they are brought to Christ, telling their friends and companions what the Lord has done for their souls. It is one way of getting the start of the devil. That period of my first love was an exceedingly joyous time. No tongue can tell the happiness of those days and nights I spent with the Lord. I used to work a bit, and then pull off my cap and pray a bit.

One night, when I was praying in the pit, a fellow-workman heard me. He thought I had met with an accident. He came to me, but I was so absorbed in my prayer that I did not notice his approach. I happened to be praying for this very man. When he found this out, he too dropped on his knees and cried, "Lord, save me!" When I turned towards him the tears were streaming down his cheeks, making white furrows on their way through the grime with which his face was covered. The Lord heard his prayer. He professed to be saved.

At the time of my conversion I owed pounds for strong drink. I determined, if God gave me strength, not to rest till I had paid the last farthing. I rejoice to say I was enabled to do so. The last I paid was to the landlord of the Irish Tavern in Congleton. We used to call that place "The hole in the wall." When I went to pay the landlord, he asked me what I would have to drink. I told him I had given up drinking and taken to praying; and that he must put that money to good interest, for he would never get any more from me. That public-house has been pulled down, and a new Town Hall built on the place where it stood. I have had the joy of preaching Christ to perishing sinners, and of praying for them on the same ground on which I used to drink and fight.

But "let him that thinketh he standeth take heed lest he fall." Take Christ's warning to heart: "Watch and pray." After enjoying the blessings of true religion for some six months, I began to think of a companion for life. Even in my unconverted state I had always said I would never marry an unconverted woman. That was due to my mother's exemplary life. One day I thought to myself: "Now, if I could only get a young woman like my mother for my wife, she would be my companion, and would be the means of saving me from mixing up with my old pals." So I prayed about it. I felt impressed to go and ask my class-leader's advice. I went and knocked at the door. His wife opened it, and said:

"Come in, Richard, my husband is inside."

"Well," I said, "you will think it strange for me to call to-night; but I have a little business on hand, and as you are my class-leader, I want your advice."

"Quite right, lad," said he; "go on."

"Do you not think that if I could meet with a godly young woman, it would be better for me to get married?—she would be a helpmate on my way to heaven."

"Yes," said he; "a good thought, lad."

"Well, do you know of any such young woman?"

"Well, that *is* a question, lad," he said. "Is it not, Hannah?"

"Yes," his wife replied, "that is a question."

After thinking awhile, he said, "Well, there's ———. If thee could'st get her, she would make a good wife. What dost thou think, Hannah?"

"Yes, I am sure she would," said his wife.

"Then," I said, "I'll go and see her at once; so good night."

Away I went to her father's house, which stood in a field about fifty yards distant from the road. I knocked at the door. It was opened by the mother.

"Good evening, Mrs. ———."

"Good evening, Richard; walk in."

I went in, and there sat the young woman's father, smoking his pipe. The daughter was ironing. What it was she was ironing I cannot say; but I will say to young men who are looking out for wives—take note of such as can wash and iron, and mend and bake. Look to that also; but above all see that she is a lover of Christ.

"Good evening," says I to the father.

"Sit thee down, Richard; glad to see thee, lad."

"Well, I have a little business on to-night. You know what sort of character I've been?"

"Yes, lad; but I'm glad to see thou'rt changed."

"And you know what sort of workman I am?"

"Yes, lad."

"Well, I am thinking of taking to myself a wife, if I can meet with a godly young woman; and I've been to my class-leader, and he tells me that your daughter here would make me a good wife, if I could get her consent and yours."

At that the daughter dropped her iron and ran out of the house; so I had the old people all to myself. The father said:

"I have nothing against it, lad."

"Nor I," said the mother; "but thou must see what she says herself."

I followed her out into the garden, and put the question. She said, "Yes; but why didn't you come and ask me first?"

So we made it up, and I made her my banker, and we kept company with each other.

Well, one night we had been to chapel, and were standing at the gate talking as two engaged people will talk before we separated. Three men came up, and I saw that they meant mischief. When they came near, they laid hands on the girl and dragged her about. When they went the length of assault on her honour, and she cried out: "O Richard, protect me!" I could no longer refrain. I off with my coat and hat, and let fly right and left. Thus I, who had been praying only a few minutes before, was betrayed into behaving like a madman. I had two of them on the ground, and had hold of the ringleader by the hair of the head, and was striking him in such rage that I believe I would have killed him had not some one stayed my hand.

I looked on what I had done as a fall from grace. I rushed without coat or hat into the public-house and called for a pint of ale. The landlady said:

"No, something is the matter. Thee shalt have no ale by my drawing."

But my old cronies sat round the table, and they offered me their glasses, saying: "Drink, Dick."

The landlady said again: "I'm sure there's something up."

The father of my girl companion jumped up from his seat in the corner, and left the house. In a short time he returned with my hat and coat, and told how his daughter had been insulted, and how I had interposed to defend her honour. I never saw men nearer using lynch law.

Morning came, and I could not go to my work, for I was ashamed. My master and other friends came to sympathize with me and to tell me I had done nothing wrong. But the fact of having gone into the public-house weighed on my mind. I felt I had fallen, and I also felt that my fall had been great. I had lost my peace with God. I had been greatly persecuted by the scoffers, and especially by the man I was to have fought with on the day of my conversion; and now that I had fallen I determined to settle accounts with him. I went to him and said:

"I have backslidden. You know how you have

taunted and insulted me. Now we must meet and settle that fight once for all."

We met about a week after. Some hundreds of people stood around us. In the first round I broke his jaw, and was pronounced the victor.

Some years afterwards I was preaching in a Primitive Methodist Chapel. The power of God filled the place. I invited any one who desired to turn to the Lord to go into the vestry. A man and woman jumped up and led the way, and some fifty others followed. In the after meeting in the chapel, I was standing on a form when the man who had been the first to go into the vestry came to me and asked permission to speak.

I said, " Yes, brother."

He turned to the people and said: " You all know me ? "

" Yes, lad."

" Well, the last time I saw Richard he broke my jaw; but to-night, God, by Richard's preaching, has broken my heart. I bless God I came in here to-night. I came in unsaved; I go home washed in the blood of the Lamb."

After my grievous fall I felt unable to remain longer at Biddulph. So I went to live at Openshaw, and worked at Clayton collieries. In my backsliding I went from bad to worse. Oh that some one had spoken to me! I became the associate of some of the worst characters in Manchester. Many a time on my bed I had fearful dreams. Here is one of those terrifying visions of the night. I dreamt that I was dead, and that my soul was lost. I thought I was carried, with my hands and feet tied, by two black creatures to the place of torment. At the mouth of the bottomless pit was a door with a great hanging lock. By that door stood One clothed in white; round his waist was a girdle at which a large key was hanging. As He spoke, I trembled from head to foot. He said: "Put him down," and they laid me on my back. He uncovered my breast, and asked, "Where is the robe I gave thee?" I said: "I've lost it." Then he took a red-hot stamp, and put it on my breast, and in letters of fire was branded the word "BACKSLIDER." I prayed Him to forgive me. He thundered the awful words, "It is too late now. Depart from me, ye cursed, into everlasting fire."

He opened the door of hell, and I was thrown in. As I dropped among the flames, there was such a yell as I never had heard before; and all the devils, with their eyes of fire, and every damned soul—some biting me, others kicking me, all crying out, "What made you come to torment us?" chased me through the caverns of the lost. Oh, how I offered, if the Lord would deliver me from that awful prison, to do what in me lay to save others from it. But no, "*Too late!*" rang in my ears again and again; and a host of the infernals chased me through the blue flames, and caught me with their blazing hands. Then I thought they cut my breast open, and began to pour a burning fluid on my heart. Still I cried, "Lord, save me!" I awoke. The bed-clothes were wet with my sweat. I thanked God it was only a dream.

But it required something more powerful than visions of hell to save me from my life of sin. Weeks after that dreadful dream I was still a slave to Satan—led captive by the devil at his will. One night I was sparring with a black man in a boxing saloon. We stood up foot to foot, and I let drive. The blow went home, and the blood ran down his black face. As I stood there looking at his blood, the Spirit of God brought that word to my mind, "The blood of Jesus Christ, his Son, cleanseth us from all sin"; and that other word, "The same Lord over all is rich unto all that call upon Him"; and that other word, "For whosoever shall call upon the name of the Lord shall be saved."

"Here, Charlie," I said, "pull off these; never again shall a pair of boxing gloves be put on my hands."

I left that saloon and went home to my lodgings; and there in my bedroom I poured out my soul to the Lord and asked Him to heal my backsliding. For answer He sent me that word, "I, even I, am He that blotteth out thy transgressions for my own sake, and will not remember thy sins." So He put a ring on my hand again, and also shoes on my feet. Next day I went to the Openshaw Wesleyan Chapel, and joined the society.

As time went on, my thoughts again began to turn towards a helpmate. The Lord had called to Himself the girl I had been engaged to in Staffordshire. At the time when my thoughts once more turned towards marriage I was sinking a shaft. We had a three-weekly shift. One week I went in at six in the morning and came out at two in the afternoon; next week I went in at two in the afternoon and came out at ten at night; and on the third week I went in at ten at night and came out at six in the morning. My class-leader lived in the same terrace. A young woman named Mary Jones lodged in his house.

A Remarkable Dream.

One day when I was in the class-leader's house he and Mary Jones were telling dreams. As a rule I have not much faith in dreams; but I thought I would tell them one I had had a short time previously. I said to Mary Jones:

"I dreamed I was out walking with you and a young man, and the young man had auburn hair."

Said the class-leader, "That's the colour of his hair."

I went on to say that I thought in my dream I was walking with Mary Jones' young woman friend, whose name I did not know.

Mary Jones said it was Sarah Bradshaw.

"Well," I went on, "we were going to Oldham Street Chapel; but on our way we came to a little chapel, and went in there instead. A woman was preaching, and she gave out as her text, 'Awake, O sword, against my Shepherd.'"

Mary Jones said, "Perhaps you will be walking with us!"

When Mary Jones got to the factory she told Sarah Bradshaw my dream. I on my part began to think about that young woman, and the more I thought, the more I felt impressed to write. By this time I had learned to write for myself; so I sent a letter to Sarah Bradshaw, asking her to meet me and take a walk with me. We all met; Mary Jones, the young man with the auburn hair, Sarah Bradshaw, and myself. We had a walk together, and arranged to meet again on Easter Sunday, and walk to Oldham Street Chapel. We met as agreed on; and as we passed along Fairfield Street we came to the little chapel that I had seen in my dream; I said:

"Let us go and see who is preaching!"

We crossed the street, and I asked the door-keeper:

"Who is the preacher here this evening?"

"Miss Buck, from Leicester," was the reply.

After that we could not but go in. I said to Sarah Bradshaw:

"If she takes the text of my dream, you will be my wife!"

Miss Buck went into the pulpit. A hymn was sung; she prayed and read; then they sang again. With no little interest I awaited the giving out of the text. *It was the text of my dream!* I sought the consent of the parents of Sarah Bradshaw to an engagement with their daughter. They were willing, and we were betrothed to each other.

A week or two after our engagement, I got my hand badly broken in a lorry wheel, and had to be taken to Manchester Infirmary. Inflammation set in, and the doctors said I must have my hand taken off. I said in my heart, "If I have my hand taken off, I shall be a cripple for life"; and I refused to allow them to cut it off. They spoke of the risk of death. I said:

"I do not fear death."

"Don't you?"

"No: Christ has taken all that away from me."

They gave me up. A young student hearing of this, offered to take my case in hand, and do what he could for me. I allowed him, and he ultimately saved my hand.

In my short Christian experience I had learnt that there is comfort and support in prayer; and it was well for me that I had. I was in no club; I was away from home and friends. I was suffering greatly: in such circumstances I was right thankful that I had God to go to. I had heard the voice of Jesus, saying, "Cast thy burden on the Lord, and He shall sustain thee"; so I laid my case before the Lord, and left it in his hands.

I also began to discover what a good thing it was that I had become engaged to a young woman who was walking with the Lord. In my affliction she proved herself a ministering angel. She sat with me in the evenings, and read the Word of God for my comfort. She prayed with me. One evening she told me that her friends in the factory had been trying to persuade her to give me up, on the ground that I should probably be a cripple for life.

"And what did you say, Sarah? I know that I am disabled for life."

She looked at me with tears of affection, and said, "What did I say, Richard? I said, 'I believe it was through the Lord that we became engaged; and I will marry him, even though I have to work to keep him.'"

Some men seek helpmates who have money; but a young woman who has Christ Jesus as her dowry has a portion that money cannot buy.

We were married in the month of January, 1853. As time went on, I found that the Lord had given me not only a praying mother; He had also given me a praying wife. All that knew her could see that she walked with God.

IV.

A Christian Working-man.

A SHORT time after our marriage we left Openshaw and went to live at New Mills, in Derbyshire. My brother George and a Mr. Edwards had entered into partnership, and had taken a small colliery, and I went to work for them. It was whilst living at New Mills I began to speak for Jesus in public. My first text in a pulpit was: "I am the Way." I cannot remember what I said; but one thing I do remember, I heartily wished myself out of that pulpit. I thought, "If only I get safe out of this, they will not catch me in a pulpit again."

The colliery proved a failure. My brother and his partner lost all their money, and had to give up the undertaking. I worked three weeks and received no wages. My wife and I were reduced to great straits. One Saturday night we sat in our little home wondering where the next meal was to come from. I thought of the good home from which I had brought my wife; I thought of our empty cupboard; and I burst out weeping. She jumped up, threw her arms around my neck, and kissing me, said:

"The Lord has promised that our bread shall be

given, and our water shall be sure; let us kneel down and pray."

We knelt down, but I was too much overcome to pray. *She* prayed. It was as though she was talking to some friend in the house. And there *was* such a Friend. Has He not said: "Where two are gathered together in my name, there am I in the midst"?

We rose from our knees and were about to retire to rest. A knock was heard at the door. I opened it. In walked our class-leader's wife with something bulky in her apron. She said:

"Mrs. Weaver, are you in need of anything?" My wife sat down unable to speak, and burst into tears. I spoke for her:

"Yes, we have not a bit of food in the house, nor money to buy any."

"Well, here is a loaf and some butter and sugar and tea; and our George has sent you a shilling, and you are to come to our house to dinner to-morrow. We were at prayer, and the master felt impressed that you needed help."

The kind sister left. My wife said:

"Now, Richard, you see that God will answer prayer: let us have faith in Him."

After thanksgiving we were again retiring. Another knock at the door.

"Who is there?"

"Open the door," was the reply.

I opened it. A hand was put in, and a man's voice said:

"Take this from the Lord—He will provide;" and five shillings were placed in my hand. To this day I know not the bearer of those five shillings; but I know the Lord was the sender.

As the work had failed we were obliged to remove. My brother and I went to Hyde, near Manchester, and there we obtained employment. One of our fellow-workmen, who was a Primitive Methodist, invited us to go with him to their meeting room. It had been a stable, with a loft above it for hay. This loft was now used as a Sabbath-school for girls. The boys were taught where the meeting was held, in the place where the horses had been. The trap-doors which led to the loft were over the pulpit, and had to be drawn up every time the pulpit was occupied. It was not much of a meeting place; but in that lowly hall many a poor sinner found his way to the foot of the cross. We threw in our lot with the congregation that gathered there.

At one of the Society meetings it was resolved to have a Band-meeting every Saturday evening. On the first Saturday I went along. No one else came. I resolved to hold the meeting, even though no earthly friend was near. I sang and prayed, and sang again, and meditated a little, and sang once more, and pronounced the benediction. When I got home, my wife asked how many had been to the meeting. I said, "Five."

"Who were they?" she asked.

"The Father, the Son, the Holy Ghost, the devil, and myself."

At one of our teachers' meetings it was proposed to expel a young woman from the school because of her sinful behaviour outside, and her unruly conduct when in the school. I thought of the woman whose story is told in the beginning of the eighth chapter of John, and I opposed the motion for expulsion. Some one said:

"Will you take the class and teach it?"

I said, "Yes."

I went home and told my wife what I had done. She said:

"That's right. I will help you to teach, and we must pray for that girl."

She proposed to invite the class to tea at our house. There were twenty-six of them. They came on a Saturday evening, and we had a grand meeting. The poor girl who had been threatened with expulsion was there among the rest. As the story of the proposal to expel her was well known, I thought it better to sound the class on the matter; so I asked if they wished her expelled. They all said, "No."

So the next Sabbath morning came, and I shall never forget it. We were reading about the wise and foolish virgins, and I was talking to them as well as I could, warning them against the danger of delay, when the young woman who had been threatened with expulsion began to cry for mercy. Then another began, and another, and another, until twenty-four of them were seeking Jesus in earnest. Before school closed that morning the twenty-four were rejoicing in the Lord. As long as I stayed in that district they kept on walking with God, and to all appearance the poor girl who had once been the worst had become the best of the lot. So was that word fulfilled, "The last shall be first."

But my fellow-workmen vexed me greatly. It is strange that while men live in sin and serve Satan they will be patted on the back and allowed to go their way without molestation: when a man is drinking and gambling and fighting, he will be hailed as a jolly good fellow; but when the Lord speaks to him and he obeys, and tries to tell his comrades how God has been gracious to him, then they turn against him and begin a course of persecution. Because I would not pay for something to drink, my fellow-workmen got me down on the ground on my back, and put a crowbar across my breast; and two men sat on it, one at one end, the other at the other, to compel me to pay. They might have sat until now as far as getting me to yield to that kind of compulsion was concerned.

They also think they may do anything to a child of God, and he must just grin and bear it. On one occasion, when working in my drift, the boy who "waggoned" for us called out:

"Richard, come here."

I went down the drift to them, and found the boy crying because a fellow-workman was trying to take the waggon from him by force. I said to him:

"Tom, you mustn't take that waggon."

He swore at me, and called me a Methodist devil, and said he wanted it and he would have it. I told him that God did not tell me to let him rob me. He cursed again, and said he would push the waggon over me.

"Nay," I said, "the Lord will not allow thee." He was in a great rage, and said he would have it.

"Well," I said, "let us see whether the devil and thee are stronger than the Lord and me."

So he began to push, and I pushed, and said, "Now Lord, now devil; now for it." And I began to sing:—

> Jesus, the Name high over all
> In hell, or earth, or sky,
> Angels and men before it fall,
> And devils fear and fly.

And the Lord and I proving stronger than the devil and he, he had to get out of the way, or the waggon would have gone over him. So I gave the waggon to the boy. Then said Tom:

"I've a good mind to smack thee on the face."

"Well," I said, "if that will do thee any good, thou canst do it." So he struck me on the face.

I turned the other cheek to him, and said, "Strike again."

He struck again and again, till he had struck me five times. I turned my cheek for the sixth stroke; but he turned away cursing. I shouted after him:

"The Lord forgive thee, for I do;" and "the Lord save thee."

This was on a Saturday; and when I went home from the coal-pit my wife saw my face was swollen, and asked what was the matter with it. I said:

"I've been fighting, and I have given a man a good thrashing."

She burst out weeping, and said, "O Richard, what made you fight?" Then I told her all about it; and she thanked the Lord I had not struck back.

But the Lord had struck, and his blows have more effect than man's. Monday came. The devil began to tempt me, saying, "The other men will laugh at thee for allowing Tom to treat thee as he did on Saturday." I cried, "Get thee behind me, Satan;" and went on my way to the coal-pit.

Tom was the first man I saw. I said, "Good morning," but got no reply. He went down first. When I got down, I was surprised to see him sitting on the waggon road waiting for me. When I came to him he burst into tears, and said:

"Richard, will you forgive me for striking you?"

"I have forgiven thee," said I. "Ask God to forgive thee. The Lord bless thee."

I gave him my hand, and we went each to his work.

After a time I heard some one coming towards me, sobbing as he came. It was Tom. He said he could not rest until he felt sure he was forgiven. He told me he had sent his wife to our house to ask my forgiveness on the Sunday, but I was out.

"O Richard," he said, "do you really forgive me?"

I said, "Yes; the Lord bless thee."

We got down on our knees. He who had wounded was graciously pleased to hear our cry and to heal; and Tom went back to his work rejoicing.

Before parting from this incident I should say that the Lord had given me an exceedingly joyous Sunday. He had also on that day given me to see some others of my class turning to the Lord. Would I have had either of these blessings had I struck back on the Saturday?

About this time I had a severe illness; but the Lord mercifully restored me to health. Those were blessed times when I worked in the coal-pit six days a week for "daily bread," and six evenings and all Sabbath for the Lord. Looking back on these days, they stand out from all the others as the happiest of my life. There were three other colliers who were Wesleyans, and we banded ourselves together and went from house to house, and held kitchen meetings for prayer. On Sabbath mornings we went round the little village in company. We would borrow a chair to stand on, and as I was the only one that could read, it was I as a rule that had to mount it as the preacher. Many of our fellow-workmen were asleep after their Saturday night's drinking; but our singing and praying generally wakened them up. Some would come out to us and sit on their heels smoking their pipes, collier fashion. Others would open their windows, and in their houses hearken to what we said. We usually sang a hymn to begin with. Then I would read a few verses of Scripture, and say, "That's what the Lord says." Then some one would pray. Our methods were primitive in the extreme. But we ran as we knew how, and the Lord graciously owned our labours. The slain of the Lord were many.

We colliers used to go to the market in Hyde on the Saturdays to buy provisions for the following week. One Saturday in 1855 I did not go to market. James Stanfield, one of the workers of whom I have been speaking, called at our house on his way home from market, and said:

"Brother Weaver, there are two men selling Bibles in Hyde Market, and they talk and sing and pray. They'll just suit us."

I asked, "Will they be there next Saturday?"

"Oi," said he, "they are going to stay a good while."

I said, "We'll go next Saturday and hear them."

When the day came we went, taking others with us.

There was a great crowd round the Bible stall—some scoffing, others listening to hear good. One of the Bible-sellers was arguing with an infidel.

The infidel was asking what God was.

The Bible-seller said, "A spirit."

Then the infidel asked what a spirit was.

The Bible-seller said God was a spirit. I thought it was time to answer the infidel fool according to his folly, so I shouted to him:

"Thou art worse than a cabbage."

"What!" he said, "you compare me to a cabbage!"

"Yes," I said, "thou art worse than a cabbage; by thine own beliefs thou art worse."

"Prove it," said the infidel.

"I will soon do that," I said; and I went on: "You believe that when a cabbage dies it goes to dung, don't you?"

"Yes."

"Well, the dung is good to put on the field for manure, is it not?"

"Yes."

"Well, you say that when you die you will become nothing; so you see you are worse than a cabbage."

He said, "Oh!" and the crowd laughed at him, and cried, "Cabbage!" and he slipped quietly away. Since then that infidel has joined with me in prayer and praise to that God whose existence he once denied.

I saw that the two Bible-sellers were exhausted, so I

said, "We will sing if you like." One of them asked us to do so, and we sang that old hymn—

> Saw ye my Saviour,
> Saw ye my Saviour and God?
> He died on Calvary,
> To atone for you and me,
> And to purchase our pardon with blood.

We joined those brethren in their good work, and we had a rich reward. Never a Saturday passed without some professing to have found the Saviour.

In 1856 it was given out that Mr. Reginald Radcliffe, a lawyer from Liverpool, would preach in Hyde market place on Good Friday. There were some thousands gathered in the market place, but Mr. Radcliffe did not turn up. As I stood in the crowd, one of the Bible-sellers espied me, and beckoned me to go up into the waggon from which they were preaching. I thought he wanted me to sing; but to my astonishment, when I got into the waggon he said to the crowd:

"The collier will speak to you."

I looked at him: I, that could scarcely read, speak to these thousands of people! I *did* tremble; but I lifted up my heart in prayer, and faced the mass of faces, and simply told them what sort of character I had been before the Lord found me, and convinced me of sin; and I told them how He revealed his love to me by giving his Son to take my place and die in my stead: and how his precious blood had taken all my sins away; and I said if Christ was able to save such a sinner as I had been, He could save the vilest sinner there. There was a cry of "Ah, Lord!" and men and women were moved by the mighty power of God, and many there and then turned to the Lord.

A few days after this Mr. Radcliffe did come to Hyde. When I first saw him he was in a large public hall on his knees pleading with God. At his suggestion we turned out and went through the streets singing and talking to the people. When we got back to the hall we found it full to overflowing, and hundreds waiting outside. There was such power in the meeting that infidels, who came there to scoff, fell down on the floor crying to God to save them.

After the meeting a few of us were invited by Mr. John Street to sup with him. During the supper Mr. Street said to Mr. Radcliffe,

"Will you give Richard a week's lodging at Liverpool?"

"Yes," said Mr. Radcliffe; "a month, if he will come."

I little thought what this was to lead to. At the request of Mr. Street, I took the place of the Bible-sellers, who had been called away to labour in other towns. After our work in the pit was over, another collier and I took our stand regularly on the Saturdays in the market place, to sell Bibles and talk to the people about Christ.

One Saturday evening in the month of April, a young gentleman came to me at the stall, and asked,

"Are you Mr Weaver?"

I said, "No."

"I beg your pardon," he said, and turned away. He came again and said,

"Is your name Richard Weaver?"

"Yes," I said.

"Well," he said, "Mr. Radcliffe has sent me to take you to Liverpool."

"You are mistaken," I said.

"No, I am not," said he; "you must go back with me."

"But, my dear sir," I said, "I cannot do any such thing. I am obliged to give my master a month's notice, or I become liable to imprisonment. Besides," I continued, "I am not qualified to go out and speak for Christ."

Mr. Street tried to persuade me to go. I made all sorts of excuses. My clothes were not of the right sort; I was not scholar enough; I did not feel called to that work; and then there was that month's notice which I was under promise to give. Mr. Street said: "I will write your master concerning that." He wrote. My master agreed to give me leave of absence for a month. But I was in great perplexity. I had a home to provide for. I was doing well in the colliery, and had the prospect of doing better. No salary was offered me. Added to that, I did not think I was qualified for such work. I knew not what to do. I only know I wanted to be guided by the Lord.

I prayed about it all Saturday evening. Sabbath morning came. I went to the early meeting. I had been presented with a new Bible. I stood with the new Bible in my hand, and said:

"Now, brethren, about leaving the coal-pit. I will shut my eyes, and open this new Bible, and I will look at the left-hand page; and if the word there points to my going, I will go; if it doesn't, I will stay in the coal-pit."

I opened my Bible. The words given were the following: "Yet have I not seen the righteous forsaken, nor his seed begging bread." I fell on my knees, and said: "Here I am, Lord, I will go."

On the Monday morning my dear wife sat weeping, with our ten-month-old firstborn on her knee as I prayed. At last she said:

"I yield to the Lord's will, and consent to your going."

So I left the coal-pit to walk by faith, and to trust in God for all I needed. Mr. Street met me at Guidebridge, gave me ten shillings, and sent me on my way with the words spoken to David, "Go, and the Lord be with thee."

V.

A Christian's Sword Exercise.

ON reaching Liverpool I was met by the young gentleman who had brought the message to me in Hyde market place, and was taken by him to Mr. Radcliffe's. There it was arranged that I was to make a start by giving out tracts in and around Chester. I received a note of introduction to Mr. A——, the superintendent of Chester City Mission. He was to supply me with the tracts, and I was to work under his direction. I was also furnished with a companion, who was to take me to Chester and introduce me to the friends of Gospel work there. On our way thither we walked as far as a farm where some friends of his lived, and with them we had dinner and a short season of prayer. We proceeded thence by rail. On our arrival in Chester my companion said to me:

"I have some friends I would like to call and see. You had better take that letter to Mr. A——, and meet me at seven o'clock by the lamp in Bridge Street, and we will have a meeting there."

I found the superintendent's house and knocked at the door. A servant opened it, and I asked if Mr. A—— was at home.

"Yes."

"Will you please to give him this note?"

She took the note in, and in a short time Mr. A—— came to the door, with my letter in his hand. He looked at me from head to foot, and said:

"You have come to give out tracts?"

I said, "Yes."

"You have, have you?"

"Yes," I said again.

"Ah!" he said; "will you meet me at such and such a place to-morrow, and I'll see what's to be done with you?"

I said, "Yes."

He then said, "Good afternoon," and shut the door.

I thought this a cold reception. I did not know where to go or what to do. I was hungry too, but shame kept me from going anywhere to buy something to eat, so I walked about till seven, and then met my friend as appointed. He took his stand on a borrowed chair, sang and prayed, and sang again, and then preached to those who had gathered around. Then I took my stand on the chair, and there began my mission work. I told the people how the Lord met me on my way to hell as He met Paul, and how for three days, like Paul, I could not see; and how at last He gave me light, and pardon, and peace. Then I sang that old hymn—

> In evil long 1 took delight,
>   Unawed by shame or fear,
> Till a new object met my sight,
>   And stopped my wild career.

And the Lord was with us. I saw tears running down the faces of many in the crowd. When the meeting was over, an old woman took me by the hand, and invited me to call and see her next day, and then she bade me " Good-night."

As my companion and I walked down the street, he asked me where I was going to stay. I told him I did not know. He told me he had secured a bed for himself at his friend's house, and then he shook my hand, and said, "Good-night! God bless thee!" *and left me!!* As he had been sent with me to care for me, I was greatly put about. I knew not what to do. It was after nine o'clock. I had not tasted food since twelve; I was an utter stranger to the city. I said to myself, " I wish I were at home."

After considering the matter, I thought I had better go and ask Mr. A——, under whom I was to work, if he could tell me of a place to stay at. He came to the door, asking:

" What is it you want ? "

" Please, sir," I said, " can you tell me where I can stay for the night ? "

" Oh yes," he said, and he wrote an address on a slip of paper, and told me to go there.

I found the street and the house. It was a low and filthy common lodging-house! And such a bed! I thought of my own clean bed at home, and was miserable. I needed no ringing up in the morning. I strolled round the ancient walls of the city till about eight o'clock, and then went to call on the old woman who had given me the invitation the night before. She gave me a hearty welcome, and an opportunity to make myself clean. She had as a lodger a young man—a joiner—who had heard me speak the night before. He asked me if I had had my breakfast. I had to confess that I hadn't. He also asked me where I had been staying. He said:

"Mrs. Evans, get him some ham and eggs."

I *did* enjoy that breakfast. Addressing his landlady again, he said:

"Mrs. Evans, if it is agreeable to you, and if he will accept my offer, he can sleep with me."

I most thankfully accepted the offer, and praised God for his kindness in thus providing for me.

At the hour appointed I went and met Mr. A——, received the tracts and instructions, and set off to the work given me to do. The races were to take place within three weeks. The tracts dealt specially with the sin of gambling; and I was expected to go through the villages around and give away these tracts, and, if possible, persuade the people not to go to the races. As I went out early in the morning, the people who had so kindly given me lodgings thought I went out to my meals. It was not so. The ten shillings that I brought with me was soon spent, and no man gave unto me. I was glad to "drink of the brook in the way." Going along a lane one day, I saw a man working among turnips in a field by the side of the lane. I begged one. That was all my food for four days. On the fourth day of my fast I was going up the street of a village, and as I went I began to sing:

> Come ye that fear the Lord
>   Unto me:
> I've something good to say
> About the narrow way,
> For Christ the other day
>   Saved my soul.

A farmer's wife heard me, and came to the gate, and said:

"Master, do you love Christ?"

I said, "Yes, I do, because He first loved me."

Then she said: "Come into the house and have a cup of tea with us."

We had tea and prayer. I told them of the mission I was engaged in. The farmer gave me two shillings, and I went on my way with my little stock replenished.

The race week came on. Mr. Radcliffe and others arrived. We held meetings every night amidst much opposition. We were pelted with paper bags full of flour and eggs, and looked fine figures, especially those who wore black coats. One night, three of us were standing before one of the principal hotels, when the betting gentlemen came out and began to push us about. While they were doing so, a man who had long hair waving on his shoulders, and who wore no hat, climbed up the lamp-post, and put his chin on the projecting rail. The lamp shone on his eyes and mouth, and his long hair and beard prevented anything else from being seen. With a hoarse voice, he shouted:

"Crucify him! Crucify him!"

The betting men looked round to see where the sound came from; and seeing nothing but the bright eyes staring at them, they bolted off as if the evil one himself were after them.

After the races I went back to Liverpool with Mr. Radcliffe, and held meetings in the open air.

One night, as I was preaching, a young woman came up to me, and said:

F

"Can Christ save me?"

I said: "Yes, for by the grace of God He tasted death for every man."

"Ah! you don't know me," she said. "I am one of those forlorn creatures."

I said, "I don't care what you are: 'He is able to save to the uttermost all that come unto God by Him.'"

"Can He save me *here*? Can He save me *now*?"

"Yes; 'Now is the accepted time: to-day is the day of salvation.' Only try Him."

She said: "If I perish, I will perish here, crying to Him to have mercy upon me."

She dropped on her knees and cried: "Lord, if Thou canst save poor prostitutes, save me *here* and save me *now*."

Presently she got up on to her feet, her eyes streaming with tears, and lifting up her hands to heaven, said:

> My God is reconciled,
> His pardoning voice I hear.

I took her with me to Mr. Radcliffe's house. She was afterwards sent to her friends at Warrington, and is now a Christian wife and mother, holding on her way to heaven, and rejoicing in a sin-pardoning God.

A few evenings later, a young man came to me at the close of an address that I had given from the words: "Be sure your sin will find you out," and told me he had run away from home, and was passing down the street where I held the meeting, on his way to take ship to America. The word had arrested him. He professed to have found mercy. I went with him to the railway station, and saw him into the train on his way back to his home.

A week before the execution of Palmer, in 1857, a fellow-labourer and I were sent to Stafford to preach there. Other brethren came to help us; and on the night before the execution we had chapels and schools open all the evening, and crowded congregations heard the word. When day began to dawn, thousands upon thousands assembled from all parts to see the poor man hanged. Platforms had been erected opposite the prison, and as much as five pounds paid for a good position. Some of us took up our stand close to the gallows, with our back to the barricade, and preached to the people. When the bell began to toll, we felt it could say, "Prepare to meet thy God," more effectively than we could say it; and we ceased speaking.

I felt I could not bear the sight of the hanging, so I shut my eyes and prayed to Him who saved the dying thief to save poor Palmer. The crowd let me know when the culprit appeared. Some howled at him; others called him a wretch, and swore at him; while others cried, "Poor fellow, the Lord have mercy on him." I stood with closed eyes, trembling and praying. The awful hush told me when the bolt was drawn. The people soon began to disperse, and we were left standing by the gallows. I opened my eyes, and had a vision that helped me to understand that word, "The end of the law." I saw a man with a cap over his face, and with pinioned arms, hanging at the end of a rope. They say, "When a man is hanged he is justified." Is it not in that sense that Christ, on Calvary's cross, is the end of the law for righteousness to every one that believeth?

From Stafford we went to Rochdale, and in the market place there we sold Bibles and held meetings. One night a sceptic came up and stood looking on. I was selling, and I said to the people:

"This is the best book in the world."

The sceptic cried, "It's the worst book in the world. There isn't a word of truth or of good in it."

I called to him to come up to the stall and prove his statements. He tried to hang back, but the people insisted on his coming forward. I asked him if he believed the Bible. He said:

"There isn't a word of truth in it, from Genesis to Revelation. I'm not going to believe a lie."

I said, "You do believe the Bible, and I will prove to the people that you do."

He said, "You can't."

I said, "Do you believe this: 'It is appointed unto men once to die'?"

"Yes," said he, "anybody knows that."

"But," I said, "the Bible says that, and you said there was not a word of truth in it.

"And now, about its badness. It says, 'Thou shalt love thy neighbour as thyself.' Is that good or bad?"

"Oh, you're bringing all the good out of it," said he.

"There, friends," said I, "he admits that there is good in it." On this he jumped down and ran off, and the crowd hooted him.

A poor man who had kept a shilling out of his wages to spend in drink was going past while I was talking to the sceptic. He stopped to listen, and the shilling was spent on a Bible instead. He went home and read it; and next time we preached he came to hear, and professed to find peace and joy in believing.

We went to Knutsford Races, and held meetings in the streets. While I was addressing a large crowd in front of a public-house, up came a man, sent by a drunken squire, and poured a gallon of ale on my head. This he did three times over. I smelt like a brewery vat.

On the great day of the races the people pushed and jostled us, and handled us very roughly. I knelt down and prayed. The heavens began to blacken; dark clouds began to appear; lightning began to flash, and the growl of the thunder was heard. The wind arose, and rapidly became a hurricane. Tents were overthrown, nut-stalls and gingerbread-stalls had their contents scattered on the ground. The rain came down in torrents, and put an entire end to the races; and they said, "It was all through that man's praying." In such a strange place was found belief in the power of prayer! Knutsford Races have never been held since.

If the hostility we met with had no bad effect on our spirits, it was somewhat hard on the appearance of our clothes. But our Provider had his own way of securing what new clothes were necessary. On one occasion when I was conducting a mission in a certain town, a gentleman kindly asked me to lodge at his house. As I sat down to the supper table, his wife, a fashionably-dressed woman, looked hard at my clothes, and then gave me a look that was anything but a look of welcome. I had not much appetite after receiving that look; nor were my spirits recovered at breakfast in the morning. By-and-by my hostess said:

"I am sorry we cannot entertain you any longer, Mr. Weaver, as we have to go to Matlock in fulfilment of an engagement which we had entirely forgotten."

"Oh, never mind, ma'am," said I; "the Lord will find me a nest to roost in somewhere."

When we rose from the breakfast table, I suggested a word of prayer. We knelt, and I made my requests known unto the Lord. Then I thanked my host and hostess, and shook hands with them, and came away. I was but a little way down the road, when a servant came running after me, saying:

"You must come back again. Missis is nearly in 'sterricks."

After a time I was persuaded, and returned. There was no word of the engagement in Matlock. Instead of that, the lady took me out and purchased for me a new suit of clothes!

After this I worked in Liverpool for some time. Mr. Radcliffe took Brunswick Hall for the Sabbath evenings, and sent me to preach there. One Sabbath evening, on my way to the meeting, a poor girl accosted me with the words, "Good evening, my dear."

"Good night, my love," said I.

"May I accompany you?" said she.

"Oh yes," I replied.

"Where are you going?" said she.

"I'm going to a dancing saloon; come and take hold of my arm."

When we got to the hall, it was crowded.

Pushing the girl before me, I said to the hall-keeper, "Make way for this young lady." I got her on to the platform, and placed her in charge of a dear sister in Christ. After I had done speaking, she fell on her knees and implored mercy from the Lord Jesus. Her prayer was heard. She was taken home by the lady into whose charge I had given her. Her mother was sent for, and the daughter who had gone astray like a lost sheep was restored to her home.

Some years afterwards I was preaching in the theatre at Leeds. A nicely-dressed woman with a baby in her arms came up to me, accompanied by a man holding a little girl by the hand. She said:

"Do you know me?"

I said, "No."

"You remember taking a young woman to Brunswick Hall one Sunday night?"

I said, "Yes."

"Well," she said, "I am that woman, and this is my husband, and these are my children; and ever since that night I have been walking with God."

She asked me to go and take tea with them.

I went, and found her husband was a local preacher; and the sower and the reaper rejoiced together.

Some of us one Sabbath evening after the meeting were returning to our lodgings singing the hymn—

> My rest is in heaven,
>   My rest is not here;
> Why then should I murmur
>   When trials are near?

> Be hushed, my sad spirit!
> The worst that can come
> But shortens my journey
> And hastens me home:
> For the Lion of Judah shall break every chain,
> And give us the victory again and again.

A policeman came up to me and said, "Stop that noise."

I said, "I shan't!"

"Then," he said, "I will make you"; and, getting hold of the neckerchief that was tied in a Lancashire slip-knot, and was therefore a running noose, he said again, "Stop it."

"No," I said, "I must sing."

He pulled the neckerchief, and brought the music to an abrupt conclusion. A rough sailor who was passing saw my fix, and knocked the policeman down. I took off my neckerchief, and have never worn one since. The policeman sprang his rattle, and another officer came to his help. One got me by the right arm, another by the left, and marched me up the street towards the Bridewell. I kept on singing—

> For the Lion of Judah shall break every chain—

and the people helped me. Passing the house of one of the brethren who had been at the meeting, he came running out without jacket or hat, to ask:

"What's the matter?"

The people said: "They are taking Weaver to prison."

He shouted, "Look up, Brother Weaver: the Lord be with thee!" and he kept shouting "Praise the Lord!"

As I wanted a companion, I said to the policemen: "One of you loose me and bring that other noisy chap with me."

So one of them said to him: "If you don't stop your noise, I will take you also."

"Glory be to God," said the brother. "Thee must just take me then; for I shall not stop praising God. Praise the Lord!"

One of the policemen caught hold of him, and marched him along with me. The brother's wife said:

"Never mind, Jack, I will fetch thy jacket and hat."

When we got into the Bridewell, we immediately fell on our knees and began a prayer-meeting. The man who kept the books said to the policemen who had run us in:

"What did you bring these men here for?"

The policeman said: "For causing a disturbance in the street."

Pointing to me as the chief offender, the book-keeper said:

"What did *he* do?"

"Why, he was shouting something about lions breaking chains, and I told him to stop, and he wouldn't; so I brought him here."

The book-keeper said: "He is with Mr. Reginald Radcliffe; you will get into a fine row over this."

He came to me with his pen in hand, and said: "You may go out."

I said: "We have been put in publicly, and we will be put out publicly."

He said: "Dear me! I never heard such a man."

I said: "You have none too many prayer-meetings here, and we'll hold one. 'Lord, save the policemen.'"

He said to our captors, "We'll have no peace all night"; and turning again to me, he said: "My good man, do go out. The next place I shall hear of you being in will be Rainhill Asylum!"

I still refused, and continued to pray and to sing. By-and-by, from behind the partition where we were, we heard some one come in and ask the book-keeper:

"Have you got a missionary here?"

"Yes, sir," said the officer.

"Will you take bail for him?"

"Bail!" said the officer. "He has been at liberty to go for the last two hours, and he won't. Do try and get him out, and I shall feel greatly obliged."

"I thought you had got the wrong man," said my friend. He came to me and advised me to go out: so I shook hands with the officers, and told them I hoped I should meet them in heaven, and bade them good-night. A few nights after this, the policeman who had taken me into custody met me and asked me to forgive him. I said:

"I forgive thee freely. Have you ever asked God to forgive thy sins?"

He said: "I'd give every hair of my head to know that my sins are forgiven, as you know that yours are forgiven."

I said: "You don't need to give anything. God gave Christ for you, and He will forgive every one that comes to Him by Jesus Christ."

The officer believed the love of God, and from that hour he helped me in every way he could.

I went with Mr. Radcliffe to Liverpool Races, to deliver tracts and to speak for Christ. A fine, stalwart, pugilistic-looking man, on his way from the station to the race-course, was accosted by one of our workers named Duckers, who pleaded with him to flee from the wrath to come. The gentleman resented the pleadings of brother Duckers. As he seemed likely to strike him, I slipped in between them, and began to talk to the stranger as lovingly as I could about Jesus his Saviour. He asked whether Jesus did not say, "If a man strike thee on the one cheek, turn to him the other also."

I said, "Yes; and if it will do you any good you can strike me."

He struck out from the shoulder, and I received a blow on my face that made me stagger; but I was enabled to turn the other cheek, and say:

"Strike again."

"Nay," he said, "I will not strike again."

I said, "Now it's my turn;" and I knelt down and prayed for his salvation. When I had done praying, and rose from my knees, he pressed two half-crowns on my acceptance, and stood by me and protected me from many who would have insulted me. Some years later, when walking down Lime Street, a stranger accosted me, and asked me if I knew him. I had to confess that I did not. He asked if I remembered a man striking me at Liverpool Races. I said I did. He said:

"I am that man. That prayer of yours for me has been heard. I can now, with you, praise God as the God of my salvation."

Not long after the Races, as my wife was unwell, I took her to my native country to see my parents. When we got to within two miles of my old home my mother met us at a stile, and threw her arms round my neck, and sobbed:

"Oh, my son, my son!"

I thought her tears were tears of joy over the return of one who had once been a heart-breaking prodigal; but I found they were tears of sorrow. My brother Thomas had been killed at work in the coal-pit at Marple, where he worked with my brother George. Such was the sad news awaiting me on my home-going. You know how it is in a country village. Everybody knows every other body. Not only that, everybody knows every other body's business. Thus, when we got to the cottage at Asterley, it was soon filled with neighbours and friends who had come in to welcome me home. Now, my mother had not thought her cottage good enough for my wife, so she had taken a room for us at the Plough Inn. It was a great trial to me to pray in the old home; but at last God gave me strength to face the trial, and so before we left the cottage for our room at the inn, I said:

"Mother, you have often prayed here for me; and now I must pray for you and father."

I took up the well-worn, well-used old Bible. It was so marked and written upon that there were some pages I could hardly read. I turned to the fourteenth chapter of John. My voice trembled as I read it. When I came to the words, "If ye shall ask the Father anything in my name, I will do it," I said:

"Mother, I'm going to ask God to save my father."

I knelt on the hearthstone on which I had often knelt in childhood while my mother with her hands on my head had pleaded with God to bless her boy; and I thanked God for all his goodness to me, and pleaded with Him to save my father. As I was praying, my father, looking to my mother, cried out:

"O Mary, what must I do to be saved? It is high time to seek the Lord's pardon for my sins, when our youngest boy is praying for me."

My mother pointed him to Jesus, and before we left for the inn, my father was rejoicing in a sin-pardoning God.

When we got to the Plough Inn the house was full of men drinking and smoking. The landlord and his wife and the company there made us heartily welcome. They offered me their cups of beer to drink with them. I said:

"Nay, I am a pump-man now."

"What! don't you drink ale?"

I said, "No, I drink water."

And I began to tell them it would be better for them if they would do likewise; and I went on to tell them how the Lord had opened my eyes and brought me to Himself. I saw tears stealing down the cheeks of not a few, and they got up to leave. I said:

"Before you go we'll have a word of prayer."

I knelt down; some of them sat; others of them knelt with me. When we arose from our knees they shook hands with me, bade me good-night, and went to their homes. The landlord and landlady and my wife and I sat in silence. I was saying to myself, "What will the landlord and his wife think of their house being cleared in this manner?"

The landlady was the first to break the silence. Looking to me she said,

"Do you think I can serve God and keep a public-house?"

I said, "No."

She said, "The vicar tells me that Mr. L——, of the 'Nag's Head,' can, and I ought."

"Yes; but he didn't tell you that when I was a boy of fifteen years of age Mr. L——, of the 'Nag's Head,' hid me, and told my poor mother, who came to inquire for me, that I was not there, though I was there, and had been there for nearly twelve hours. No, no, Mrs. E——, it cannot be done. *You must give up selling that which destroys earthly homes, or there will be no heavenly home for you.*"

She shouted out, "John!"

I heard a voice from another room: "Yes, ma'am."

"Come here," said the landlady. A man appeared.

"John," she said, "fetch a ladder and pull down the sign." That very hour it was done.

Next morning an old toper came on the sly to get a drink. The landlady said:

"Go and look over the door—the sign is down."

"So it is," said he.

"Yes," she said, "I've done with drink-selling; so you needn't come here any more."

At the close of the service which I conducted in the Primitive Chapel in the evening, our landlord and his wife were among the thirty-five who came to the form to decide for Christ.

I went with Mr. Radcliffe to the Chester Races for the second time. One morning, as I stood giving out tracts, I saw a gang of men from Staffordshire. As they drew near they recognised me. I heard one say, "Hullo! here's 'Undaunted Dick.'"

"Good morning, Undaunted," said he.

"Good morning," said I.

"How art going on?"

"First rate, praise the Lord."

"Now, Weaver, how much hast thou gained by serving the Lord?"

"How much hast thou gained by serving the devil?"

"Well," he said, "I've won two whole streets of houses by horse-racing; and if I win to-day I shall have another street."

"I have gained far more than that," said I.

"How is that?" he asked.

"Well, Tom, I will tell thee. I have become heir to an inheritance incorruptible, undefiled, reserved in heaven for me; and when thy bricks and mortar have crumbled into dust, my inheritance will be safe and secure."

"Oh," said he, "good morning."

Some years afterwards, while holding a mission in Dublin, I one day in Sackville Street met a man whom I thought I knew. His clothes and his shoes were the worse for wear, and he looked anything but happy. It was Tom. I stopped and asked:

"What brings you here?"

"Ah, Weaver," he said, "this meeting is providential. Wilt lend me a shilling?"

"Why, where's thy two streets, Tom?"

"Gone," he replied; "I have lost all, and I am here out of the way of the policeman."

I urged him to look after his interest in the inheritance that fadeth not away, gave him half-a-crown, and went on my way recalling that word, "Godliness is profitable unto all things, having the promise of the life that now is, and of that which is to come."

One night, during those Chester Races, we stood under a lamp in Bridge Street, near a large hotel that was much resorted to by betting men. Some of the gamblers gave five pounds to a man who was selling a list of the races to pull the preacher from the chair. At the time he set about the attempt a Baptist minister was preaching. As the race-card seller came pushing and elbowing his way towards the speaker, a rough, hard-set, resolute-looking Lancashire man, hailing from Bolton, said:

"What art doing?"

He replied, "I am going to pull that man off the chair."

"Nay," said the Lancashire man, "theau shalt na: my feyther and mother are good people i' Bowton, and I'm a bad son; but these are good men. Theau shalt na pu' him deawn."

The Chester man said, "If yo dunno stand back, I will knock thee down."

"Two can play at that game," said the other.

The race-card man struck him, and the other instantly struck back.

As soon as the fight commenced, the Baptist minister jumped down from the chair, and away he ran. Where he ran to, I do not know. If he continued at the rate at which he started, he is far past Jericho long ere this. A ring was formed round the fighters. Mr. Radcliffe asked a policeman who was looking on to stop the fight. He refused to interfere. The betting men in the hotel windows shouted:

"Give him fair play."

"Yes," said the little Bolton man, "he shall have fair play; and when I have done with him, one or two of you gentlemen can come down, and I'll serve you the same."

And he turned to his work, and soon finished it in a workmanlike manner.

Mr. Radcliffe jumped on the chair, and began to speak about Jesus. In a twinkling the policeman who refused to stop the fight commanded him to desist. He refused. The policeman pulled him off the chair. Another of our workers, named William Brown, instantly mounted it. The brave policeman took hold of him and pulled him down also. I jumped up. The policeman looked at me; but, as he had not got three hands, he could do nothing more; so he marched his prisoners off to the Bridewell, while I preached to the crowd. Presently I saw him coming round the corner of the street, wiping the perspiration from his brow. Coming to me, he said:

"Are you going to stop?"

I said, "Nay, not till I have had my say; and if you touch me before I have had my say, the Lord may take an arm from you."

He said nothing, but stood looking at me till I had finished. Then I jumped down and took the policeman by the arm, and we marched up the street, with hundreds following us. I began to sing the old battle song—
> For the Lion of Judah shall break every chain.

The crowd took it up. I kept nudging the policeman in the ribs with my elbow.

"Sing, man," I said.

He said, "Come along."

I nudged him again and said, "Sing up, man."

So we went to the Bridewell. When we got inside I said to Mr. Radcliffe and Mr. Brown, who had been taken there before me, "We'll have a word of prayer."

Mr. Radcliffe laughed and wept.

Mr. Brown said "Amen."

I prayed. By-and-by came in Major T—— with the chief of police, and they held a consultation together. A number of constables were inside. After a time there was a knock at the door.

"Who's there?" asked a constable.

"I have brought a supper for the missionaries."

Cold ham, cold fowl, cold salmon, and other good things were brought in in abundance. Almost immediately there was another knock. It was a second "supper for the missionaries." In walked a man in livery—white tie and knee-breeches—carrying a tray covered with white cloth, which when removed exposed to view another nice supper. A third came. I tell you, friends, I never had so many suppers in one night in my life! I could not help thinking times had changed since Paul and Silas were put in prison for speaking of Jesus.

After our suppers Mr. Radcliffe was called before Major T——, and the following conversation took place.

"What is your name?"

"Reginald Radcliffe."

"What business?"

"Solicitor."

"Oh! Where from?"

"Liverpool."

"Will you give bail?"

"No. We have been put in publicly, and we will be put out publicly."

"Lock him up," said Major T——.

The constables refused, and Mr. Radcliffe went and sat down. A similar talk took place between Major T—— and Mr. Brown, and he also went and sat down.

Then I was called up.

"What's your name?"

"A sinner saved by grace."

"Pooh! pooh! Tell me what your name is."

"A sinner saved by grace."

"But where do you come from?"

"The City of Destruction."

"Pooh! pooh! Where is your home?"

"In heaven."

"Will you give bail?"

"Bail? Why, do you want me to give bail twice? The Lord Jesus Christ gave bail for me above eighteen hundred years ago, and I am not going to give bail again."

"Lock him up," said the major; and in my case also the constables refused. Just then in came Dr. D——, another magistrate, shook hands with us, and said to Major T——:

"If you put these men in damp cells, I shall hold you responsible for any ill effects that may ensue. As one of them is weakly you will have to give them beds and blankets."

The major said, "Doctor, will you give bail for them?"

"Yes," said the doctor; and he did it.

Coming to us again, he asked Mr. Radcliffe to go out with him. Mr. Radcliffe thanked him, but said that as we had been publicly put in, our out-going must also be public. I overheard the major say to the chief constable, "I wish I had had nothing to do with this affair." The chief of police told his officers to go outside and clear away the crowd from the door. When the door was open, the chief constable got hold of Mr. Radcliffe, and pulled him towards it. Then he took hold of Mr. Brown, and did likewise with him. Then he pulled me in behind Mr. Brown. Then Major T—— and the chief constable got in behind me, and pushed all three of us right out on to the street, in the sight of the assembled thousands, and we returned to our stand in Bridge Street and sang:

Praise God from whom all blessings flow.

Next day Mr. Radcliffe sent a special engine, carriage, and brake, to Birkenhead for a barrister to plead for me. After a trial lasting four hours and a-half we were acquitted.

VI.

Incidents in the Warfare.

AT THE ELEVENTH HOUR.

ONE Sunday afternoon, when labouring in Tarvin, a gentleman came and asked me to visit a sick man.

"Where does he live?" I asked.

"At Stamford Bridge," was the reply.

"How far is that?"

"About two miles."

"I have to preach here to-night: how can I get there and back?"

"I will drive you in my gig."

I got ready and went. To my surprise I was driven up to a public-house. My friend told me it was the publican who was ill. I knocked at the door. No one answered. Hearing conversation, I walked in. There sat men drinking; the servant-girl was talking and laughing with them, as if neither death nor sickness was near. I asked the girl if there wasn't some one ill in the house. She said:

"Yes, master is ill; you will find him upstairs."

She did not so much as rise to show me where the stair was; but it was an old-fashioned house, and I soon found the stair, and began to walk up. When I got to the landing I heard some one speaking, but was at a loss to know from which room the sound came.

Presently I discovered it was the room to my right. As I paused in the doorway, an agonized voice from the bed was saying:

"Look at me, my dear wife and children; I am dying: I fear I shall be lost. Can you tell me what I must do to be saved?"

His weeping wife and children sobbed out, "No."

On the right of the dying man sat two sisters. To them he addressed the same earnest appeal:

"Can you tell me what I must do to be saved?"

"No, brother," said they; and they wept and sobbed aloud.

A man of some fourscore years sat at the foot of the bed. To him the dying man next turned with his piteous enquiry:

"Father, can you tell me what I must do to be saved?"

"No, my boy, I wish I could," was the weeping father's reply.

I thought it was time for me to walk in. They looked at me, but did not ask who I was nor where I had come from. The sick man put out his hand, and said:

"Sir, I am dying; and the minister tells me that as I have been baptized and confirmed, and have taken the last rites of the church, and been prayed for, I must just rest content: but I cannot, for I fear I shall be lost. Can you hold out any hope for me, sir?"

I said, "Yes, thank God, I can. I have come with some promises spoken by the Lord Jesus Christ, who died for you."

I opened my Bible and began to turn to the tenth chapter of Romans. As I was doing so, the dull eyes of the publican brightened, and the heavy cloud passed away from his countenance as he asked:

"Oh, is there a promise for poor G—— ?"

I said: "Yes; but if I read it to you, will you believe it?"

For answer he told me what a character he had been for fighting and everything that was bad. I told him a little of my own evil history. He asked:

"Have you been as bad as that?"

"Yes," I said, "and *I* have found pardon."

The execution of poor Palmer was very vivid at that time in the minds of all in that neighbourhood; so I read: "Christ is the end of the law for righteousness to every one that believeth." I reminded him that the execution was the end of the law to Palmer. The offended law was satisfied when the penalty had been paid. I showed him that the law of God had no such claim on Christ as the law of England had on Palmer; and yet He paid the death penalty. To whom then is Christ the end of the law? According to the New Testament, "To every one that believeth." Then I read to him the verses that follow: "Moses describeth the righteousness which is of the law, That the man who doeth those things shall live by them. But the righteousness which is of faith speaketh on this wise: Say not in thine heart, Who shall ascend into heaven? (that is, to bring Christ down from above); or, Who shall descend into the deep? (that is, to bring up Christ again from the dead). But what saith it? 'The word is nigh thee, even in thy mouth, and in thy heart; that is, the word of faith which we preach, that if thou shalt confess with thy mouth the Lord Jesus, and shalt believe in thine heart that God hath raised Him from the dead, thou shalt be saved.'" Then I quoted John iii. 16, and tried to show him how Christ with his finished work on Calvary was God's offered gift to him and to me, inasmuch as the offer is to " whosoever believeth."

He said: " Is that in my Bible ? "

I said: " Yes, it is in your Bible."

He said to his elder child: " You read it to me, and I will believe it."

She lifted the family Bible that lay on the bed, and opened it: but tears so bedimmed her sight that she sobbed out:

" O father, I cannot read it; but it must be there, or he would not say it is."

The publican's younger child stepped forward, wiped his eyes, and said:

" Father, I will read it." He found the place. He read the life-giving words: " God so loved the world, that He gave his only-begotten Son, that whosoever believeth in Him should not perish, but have everlasting life."

The publican clapped his hands, and said:

" Thank God, I can rest contented now. God so loved me that He gave his Son to die for me."

What a scene of weeping and rejoicing! The publican had not been out of bed for weeks; but whilst I was praying, he somehow got on his feet on the floor, and put his arms round his wife's neck, and said:

" It's done me more good than all the medicine. The blood of Jesus Christ cleanseth me from all sin. Praise the Lord!"

He said to me. "The devil wanted to have poor G——; but the Lord has saved me!"

He was so far restored in health that he was able to go in a cab to Chester, and tell his friends what the Lord had done for his soul. Some time afterwards he asked his wife to write me. I have that letter. It is adorned with teardrops as the fields in early summer are adorned with daisies. His message was as follows:

"Tell Richard Weaver poor G—— has got the victory."

Not long after, he died, triumphing in Christ.

The Real Proprietor.

On one occasion, when travelling from Chester to Liverpool, I was led into a somewhat amusing conversation with an old gentleman farmer who entered the train at Warrington. He at once became very communicative, and in a short time the conversation took the following turn:

"Do you see that house over the river?" he asked.

"Yes," I said.

"Well, I can remember when the gentleman who lives there had hardly a sixpence that he could call his own; and now that house and all this land belongs to him."

"Nay, friend," said I, "you are mistaken. This land belongs to my Father."

"Your Father, sir?"

"Yes. I am a King's son."

The old gentleman looked astonished, and asked:

"Where do you come from?"

"From the City of Destruction."

"Where's that? It is not in this country, is it? Is it not over the water?"

"Yes," I said, "it's over the water" (an allusion to baptism).

"Let's see," said the old gentleman. "Our country has a Queen, not a King."

"Yes," I said; "but my Father is a King."

"Dear me!" said the old gentleman.

"Yes," I said, "and all this land on each side of the railway, from Warrington to Liverpool, belongs to my Father."

"Nay," he exclaimed. "Then he must have leased it. Hasn't he?"

"They have leased it of my Father," said the King's son.

"Dear me!" said the other, "I never heard of such a thing as that."

"All Cheshire," continued the King's son, "belongs to my Father."

"Nay, I am sure that's a lie," said the other, indignantly. "I've got a farm in Cheshire, and I'm going now to Liverpool to settle about my will."

"I don't care. The farm belongs to my Father."

"I'm sure it don't."

"And all the money in your pockets belongs to my Father."

"It's a downright lie," said the old gentleman, now quite angry, and he looked at me as if he thought I had just broken loose from some asylum; but he said:

"Tell me what your Father's name is."

"Well," I said, "He is called by different names; but I call Him, 'God is love.'"

The old gentleman told me he hadn't thought of these things. I talked to him about the seriousness of the situation for him when, according to his own confession, he was on his way to make his will, and as yet was not able to call God his Father. He confessed his desire for a Father in heaven. We knelt in the railway carriage. He prayed the publican's prayer. God was pleased to hear his cry. We got out at Garston, and got on to the top of the omnibus to ride to Liverpool; and the old farmer could do nothing else but praise God and tell our fellow-passengers how he had found Christ in the railway carriage. When we parted company he pressed half a sovereign on my acceptance. As I took it I could not help saying, "Didn't I tell you the money in your pockets belonged to my Father?"

At the Fair.

Having been appointed Town Missionary at Prescot, I was led, at the time of the Fair, to ask my brethren to help me to make an attack on the tomfooleries that were carried on in the market-place. In the midst of the travelling theatres, boxing saloons, swing boats, shooting galleries, and shows of various descriptions we took our stand, and began to sing:

> Come, ye that love the Lord,
> And let your joys be known;
> Join in a song with sweet accord,
> And thus surround the throne.

They attempted to drown our voices. One theatre company called a band to their aid. We kept to the one hymn, singing it over and over again. On one side there were showmen's bells ringing, drums being beaten, cymbals clashing, rattles rattling, and the band playing. On the other side only the unaided voices. For two hours the contest proceeded. By-and-by the drummers began to show signs of fatigue; first one hand got cramped, then the other. It was the same with the musicians; the cramp got in amongst their fingers. At last they gave in, and our voices held the field. A gentleman came to me, and said he had taken the Town Hall for us. In less than ten minutes it was packed in every corner. The power of God came down upon the gathering; saints were baptized with the Spirit; sinners were saved.

On the following evening my fellow-labourers and I again took our stand in the market-place. No one was entering the shows or theatres. One of the merry-andrews, with painted face, challenged me to go on his stage and hold a controversy with him. It was just what I wanted. He thought to have some sport with me; but he soon stood before the people confuted and silenced. At last he asked:

"Would you give me a loaf of bread if I wanted one?"

I said, "Yes."

"Then I do want one," said he.

"Come along, then," said I; and I took him by the arm, and we went down off the stage and through the crowd and up the street to the baker's shop. I bought two loaves and gave them to him.

"Let me pay for them," said he.

"Nay," said I; "but kneel with me, and I'll pray with thee."

As I prayed he wept. Next morning he came to my house, and asked me to forgive him. Ere he left he professed to have found Christ.

One of the showmen, at the close of the Fair, complained that, while he had taken £10 at the Fair a year before, he had not taken 10s. at this Fair. He laid the blame at my door. When pulling down his show, one of his children was heard asking:

"Are you going to Newton Races, father?"

"No," he said; "it's no use going there. That preacher is going."

From the Mother to the Son.

One day a priest knocked at the door of the house of one of the members of his flock, called "Old Irish Mary," and asked her if it was true that she "had joined Dicky Weaver's lot."

"Yes, Father," she said; "you told me to go to the Mother: and I have prayed to her all these years, and have never derived any benefit. That man told me to go to the Son of God, and I went, and He has made me free. I have not got my scapular over my shoulders now; I have burned it. I do not bow before the crucifix now; I have burned it also."

The priest got angry, and cursed her eating and cursed her drinking; cursed her waking and cursed her sleeping; cursed her lying down and cursed her standing up; cursed her eyes and cursed her ears; cursed her hands and cursed her feet. What an awful prayer! Mary heard it out, and said:

"You have only wasted your breath, for the Lord has set a hedge about me; a hedge so high that your curse cannot get over it; a hedge so thick that your curse cannot get through it; a hedge so deep-set that your curse cannot get under it: and all the time you have been cursing, God has been blessing."

The priest beat a retreat, and Mary went on her way rejoicing.

In the Public-House.

Passing a beer-house one day with a friend, we heard a tap on the window. We turned to look, and saw a man beckoning us in. The landlord of that very place had boasted that if ever I dared to enter his public-house, he would speedily put me to the door; but having received an invitation from those within, I thought it well to enter, and ask what they wanted.

"Oh, nothing," said the man who had tapped on the window.

"But," I said; "you called me in, didn't you?"

"Yes," he said.

"Well," I said; "you know I don't drink, and you know my business in Prescot is to warn sinners to flee to Christ." And I began to plead with them to leave their sins before it was too late.

We knelt to pray. I had noticed a large bull terrier dog in the room. As I knelt on one knee, I felt the dog pass under the other knee, and growl. I knew enough about dogs to know that if its tail was hanging down, it might bark but it wouldn't bite. I opened my eyes to see if it meant to bite me. One glance convinced me that the Lord had muzzled the dog as well as the men. So I continued my prayer. One old woman began to cry for mercy. My friend began to shout, "Glory, Hallelujah!"

I was told afterwards that the publican came, with his wife, to the door of the room, and looked in at us on our knees; but, instead of turning us out, they went out themselves, and hid themselves in the tool-house at the foot of the garden. One wonders what they were afraid of. I was also told that an officer from the police station on the other side of the street came across to find out the meaning of the shouting, and, having seen, went back to his chief and reported:

"It's only Mr. Weaver praying."

"Then come in and shut the door, or we'll have him praying here directly."

"Nelly, I've got it!"

While Town Missionary of Prescot I visited and preached in many of the villages around. On one occasion in Haydock my text was, "My Spirit shall not always strive with men." In the audience was a man who was a great dog-fancier and pigeon-flyer. The word of the Lord took such hold upon him that he did not know what to do with himself.

When he got down into the coal-pit next morning he did not dare to begin work till he had prayed. Even after prayer he was afraid to stay, lest the roof should fall on his head. He went home and sat in the house all day sighing, "Oh dear, what must I do?" The next day was passed in the same way. His wife and neighbours thought he had gone mad. On the following day he again tried the coal-pit, but was compelled to return to his home. He got hold of the Bible and hymn-book and went upstairs with them, and cried to the Lord to have mercy upon him. Opening the hymn-book, he began to read the first words that caught his eye. They were as follows:

> My God, I know, I feel Thee mine,
>   And will not quit my claim
> Till all I have is lost in Thine,
>   And all renewed I am.
>
> I hold Thee with a trembling hand,
>   But will not let Thee go
> Till stedfastly by faith I stand
>   And all thy goodness know.

When he had got thus far, the light broke in on his darkness; and he ran to the top of the stairs and shouted, "Nelly, I've got it! Nelly, I've got it! I've got Jesus!"

He praised God so loudly that the neighbours came to see what was the matter. They found his wife and children weeping, because they were under the impression that he had gone out of his mind. At that time he had some money in the Savings' Bank. As one result of his conversion he drew all his money and gave it to the poor. He is now—at the time of writing—an accredited local preacher among the Wesleyans, and is one of the choicest men I know.

"BUT IF NOT—BLOT MY NAME OUT OF THY BOOK."

From other places came the cry, "Come over and help us." At last it became so urgent that I saw it was not the Lord's will that I should stay in Prescot, so I again set out under pillar-cloud guidance. God's Spirit was working. At one place where I conducted meetings for a fortnight, five hundred gave in their names as having received God's pardon during the mission. Thirteen marriages of men and women who had been living together were part of the results of these meetings.

At one place a sorely-tried woman begged me to join her in prayer for her husband. I pointed out to her the word, "If two of you shall agree as touching anything ye shall ask, it shall be done"; and said I would go home and go into my bedroom and spend an hour pleading with God for her husband, if she would go to her home and do likewise. I did as I had promised, and went out afterwards with my host for a walk. We went in the direction of the woman's home. When we got within view of the house, we saw a crowd standing under the window. When we drew near I heard the woman at prayer. As I looked at the faces of the crowd, I saw that all were serious; some of them were weeping. I heard the words, "Now, Lord, if Thou wilt not save my husband, blot my name out of thy book." I did not then know that the words were in the Bible; so I was somewhat astonished at her. At our next meeting, nearly a hundred professed to find peace. I was going from pew to pew seeking the slain of the Lord, when I noticed a man who looked exceedingly miserable. Addressing him, I said:

"Master, have you got Christ?"

"No."

"Do you want Christ?"

"Yes."

"When do you want Him?"

"I want Him now."

"Well, friend, every step out of that pew is a step towards Calvary. Come along."

I got him into the vestry. He fell down as if struck with a hammer. It was the old cry, "God be merciful to me a sinner!" I went back to the chapel praising

God. My praying friend met me with "Glory be to God! Do you know the man you took into the vestry? It was my husband!"

She went to the vestry. She dropped on her knees beside her praying husband. She began to plead with God, saying, "Now, Lord, I bring Thee to the test. Save my husband to-night, or blot my name out of thy book." Some said "What a reckless prayer!" She heeded not, but kept on pleading until her husband shouted:

"Rachel, the Lord has pardoned my sins!"

He threw his arm round her neck and kissed her, and they praised God together. When last I heard of them they were walking hand-in-hand towards heaven.

A Word to the Choir.

God's Spirit was abroad in the land, making things possible that, but for his descent in power, would only have issued in humiliation. It was no unusual thing to have on an average a hundred professed conversions for every night that a mission lasted. While things were so I was asked to preach in a chapel where the praise was led by a choir chosen more for their good voices than for their godly lives. Beside the chapel was an ale-house, into which numbers of the choir used to retire when the preacher gave out the text.

I had been asking the Lord for guidance concerning this matter; and when I got into the pulpit I felt that the Lord was with me. I took my text, and turned round and deliberately preached to the choir direct. They fell before the word, and instead of going to the ale-house, they went to the schoolroom to be dealt with as anxious inquirers, while I continued the service.

In the Dancing Saloon.

One night, while I was conducting a mission in Darlaston, I was making my way, somewhat late, to my lodgings; when, as I was passing a public-house, I heard music and dancing. I said to my companions:

"I will go into the dancing room."

"Nay," said one, "they won't let you."

"Well, I'll try," said I.

I walked upstairs. A man stood at the door of the room, and I gave him sixpence to let me in. One was scraping a fiddle, another was twanging a banjo, and the dancers were whirling and wheeling round each other.

I knelt in the middle of the floor and began to pray. The dancers at once made for the door, and ran helter-skelter downstairs as if the devil was after them. The fiddler, the banjo-player, and I were left alone. The banjo was laid on the floor: its owner jumped on it, smashing it to pieces; then he dropped on his knees beside me and cried to God for mercy. The fiddler was weeping. The landlord came to the door, with a gun in his hand, swearing he would shoot me. His wife was wrestling with him to get the gun out of his hands. At last she got possession of it, and I left the house. As I passed the house on the following evening, I noticed it was closed. I have been told that never again has a dance taken place in that house.

"Leave off Talking, and Pray."

A collier there, who had the reputation of being the wickedest man in the pit in which he worked, was convicted by the word. He came to my lodgings to ask,

"What must I do to be saved?" I pointed him to the finished work of Christ. No light came. At last he said:

"Leave off talking, and do kneel down and pray for me. I've had enough of talking."

He dropped on his knees himself and prayed. Jesus heard his cry, and brought him "into the banqueting house."

A Hunter for Souls.

One day I was standing on a bridge over a brook. I heard the hunter's horn. Very soon I saw the hounds coming towards me in full cry. Before they got near, a hare ran up the field close by, and then down the side of the brook; every now and then leaping into the water, as if to throw the dogs off the scent. When the hounds came up they were at fault. The foremost hunter came to me and said, "Have you seen the hare?"

"Yes," I said.

"Which way did she take?"

"You must find that out," said I; and I went on to say, "Man, I am a hunter for souls. Death on the pale horse with all the dogs of hell is upon your track. They are pursuing you as you are pursuing the hare; and unless you flee to Christ, you will lose your soul."

"Oh!" he said, and rode away.

Shortly afterwards, when preaching, I made use of the incident. The arrow found the heart of a drinking, gambling, sporting man, who was in the audience. That night he sprang out of bed in terror, screaming,

"Lord, save me! Lord, save me!"

His wife jumped up and asked him what was the matter.

"Oh," he said, "I thought Death on the pale horse was after me."

He lay down again; but scarcely had he fallen asleep when the same dreadful vision returned. Once more he cried to God to save him. Again he fell asleep, and a third time the dream came. He cried out:

"If I don't begin to pray, I shall be in hell before day."

In the darkness of the night the two of them knelt in prayer, and the poor, death-hunted sportsman, by betaking himself to the River of Life, was enabled to baffle the hell-hounds that were crying out for his soul.

VII.

The London Campaigns.

WITH THE CHIMNEY SWEEPS.

IN the beginning of 1860 I received an invitation to speak at a meeting of chimney sweeps in London. I thought it a great thing to be invited to speak in London, and supposed that I would have to put on my best manners. I was in such fear and trembling, that all the way up I kept praying to the Lord to give me the needed help and guidance. The meeting was held in a little hall in Euston Road. We entered it by a narrow, dark staircase. The congregation was in keeping with the room and its surroundings.

I had seen rough meetings in my day, but I was face to face with a much rougher lot than ever I had seen before. Ladies and gentlemen were there to try and make them happy. Lord Congleton was chairman After the sweeps had been served with tea, they swore at and quarrelled with each other so fiercely, that I began to think there would be a general fight. The chairman got up and cried: "Order, gentlemen." They paid not the slightest attention to his appeal. Other gentlemen got up and attempted to calm the storm. It seemed as easy to quiet hyenas. It came into my mind to sing to them; so I said to one of the gentlemen:

"I think I could get them to be quiet."

He said: "You don't know what a meeting of London sweeps is."

The efforts to restore order continued. It was in vain. At last one of the gentlemen turned to me and said:

"If you think you can quiet them, you are at liberty to try."

I rose and shouted at the top of my voice:

"Order, boys, and I'll sing you a song."

They cried: "Hear, hear."

I said: "Now, Jim, thee keep Jack quiet"; and they fell to work to keep each other quiet; and I sang the hymn:

> Glory be to God on high!
> Jesus Christ is passing by,
> God is reconciled.

They took up the chorus and sang it with might and main. When the hymn was finished, I said:

"Men, these gentlemen want to speak to you now."

One of the gentlemen began to speak; but the uproar also began again. They would not listen. So I sang the hymn:

> On the other side of Jordan;

and again appealed to them to hear the speakers. Another gentleman began to speak; but they would not give him a hearing. A third time I got up to sing, and I sang the hymn:

> Come sing to me of heaven
> When I'm about to die.

While I was singing that third hymn, I noticed tears running down the cheeks of some of them; so when the hymn was finished, I began to speak to them. The power of God came down on the meeting. I got down among them, and went from seat to seat, putting my hand on the head of such as were weeping, and speaking a word of comfort to them.

The place was very hot. The sweat was running down my face. I put up the hand that had been on the sweeps' heads to whisk off some of the perspiration. My hand left my face covered with soot! The friends on the platform laughed at me. That did not trouble me in the least, as souls were being saved. When the meeting was over, the soot was easily washed away.

USING THE ENEMY'S GUN.

Mr. William Carter, a devoted servant of Christ, thought he might make some little use of my past life in the way of exciting interest in the meetings; so on hand-bills and posters he issued the following notice:

To Prize-Fighters, Dog-Fanciers, and Sporting men of all sorts:

COME AND HEAR

RICHARD WEAVER,

KNOWN AS

"UNDAUNTED DICK,"

the converted prize-fighter, from the mines of Lancashire. He will sing and preach in Cumberland Market, Regent's Park, on Sunday morning, June 3rd, at eleven o'clock: and in the evening at six o'clock. He will narrate his wonderful conversion, and other striking circumstances of his life. He will also sing and preach in the same place every evening the following week.

THE UNLEAVENED BREAD OF SINCERITY AND TRUTH.

Into Mr. Weaver's own narrative we interject an account of those meetings from the pages of *The Revival*.

We have listened to him (Richard Weaver) with unbounded pleasure. The salvation which is in Jesus is to him a river to swim in (Ezek. xlvii. 5). *Somewhat startling indeed is the originality both of his words and deeds;* but wait it out, and you'll say, It has been good to be here. "Salvation," he cries aloud, "isn't in sacraments. Many go from the communion-rail to hell. It isn't in having the Bishop's hand laid on your head. It isn't in going under the water. It isn't in groans, and tears, and prayers. It's in the blood of Christ. Look to Him! I'll get out of sight," and he hides himself beneath the extemporized pulpit.

"Soul-saving blood; sin-cleansing blood; peace-speaking blood; devil-confounding blood." What our gracious Lord loves is sincerity of purpose and singleness of eye; and Richard Weaver keeps the feast with the unleavened bread of sincerity and truth. He longs and with all his heart labours for the salvation of souls. "My friends tell me I'm killing myself. I have come to London because I love you working men: and now I'll preach to you, if you carry me from this waggon to the grave.

"A kind brother said he would pay my fare to London, if I could trust the Lord to keep me when I got there; and, bless the Lord, I *can* trust Him. Hold up your hands all who are on the Lord's side. Now all who are anxious, hold up your hands. Who'll volunteer? Don't be ashamed. One hand is up. Bless the Lord. Another hand—another. Come up here, you dear souls, and we'll pray with you, and talk to you. Now all kneel down. If you would get to heaven, you must kneel. They get on best that kneel most."

Let it not be supposed that levity accompanies all this. Indeed no. We have attended no meetings more solemn nor more rich in results.

One evening his text was: "They shall return to Zion with songs." He declared he had always been fond of singing; but, "the songs I used to sing are not the songs I love now. I used to sing 'We won't go home till morning.' The landlady likes to hear that song. I've sung that five nights together and spent £14 on one spree, and got turned out at the end; she wouldn't trust me for a quart. But I've learned better songs. I'll tell you some of them. Here's one:

> Oh, happy day, that fixed my choice;

and here's another:

> There is a fountain filled with blood."

The speaker quoted with marvellous rapidity, but without the semblance of irreverence, at least a dozen hymns or portions of hymns, some of which he sang, the meeting taking up the chorus. Then with wonderful tenderness and pathos of voice and manner he related the following anecdote:

I knew a collier in Staffordshire who had one dear little girl, the last of four or five. The child was the light of his eyes, and as he came from the pit at night, she used to meet him at the door of his cot to welcome him home. One day when he came home to dinner he missed his little darling; and going into the house with his heavy coal-pit clogs his wife called him upstairs. The stillness of the place and her quiet voice made his heart sick; and a foreboding of evil came upon him. His wife told him they were going to lose their little lamb; she had had an apoplectic fit, and the doctor said she couldn't live. The tears made white furrows down his black face as he leaned over his dying darling; but she said, "Daddy, sing

> Here is no rest—is no rest."

"No, my child, I can't sing. I'm choking; I can't sing."
"Oh, do, daddy, sing 'Here is no rest.'"
The poor fellow tried to sing (*preacher sings*)—

> Here on the earth as a stranger I roam,
> Here is no rest—is no rest.

But his voice couldn't make way against his trouble. Then he tried again, for he wanted to please his little girl (*preacher sings*)—

> Here are afflictions and trials severe,
> Here is no rest—is no rest;
> Here must I part with the friends I hold dear,
> Yet I am blest—I am blest.

Again his voice was choked with weeping; but the little one whispered:

"Come, daddy, sing 'Sweet is the promise';" and the poor father went on again:

> Sweet is the promise I read in thy Word,
> Blessed are they who have died in the Lord;
> They have been called to receive their reward,
> There, there is rest—there is rest!

"That's it, daddy," cried the child; "that's it"; and with her arms round her father's neck, she died happy in the Lord.

We resume Mr. Weaver's own narrative.

WHAT DOEST THOU HERE?

While preaching in London I had a visit from an uncle of my wife. He had been living for some years in America, and had come to England on a visit to his relatives. Having come up with a Manchester gentleman to London, and put up at the Robin Hood Hotel, he sent me an invitation to call on him there. When I called, nothing would please them save my spending the day with them. I agreed to go with them. The first place they took me into was a large room brilliantly lighted up with gas, although it was a bright summer day. There was a stage, with a row of footlights along it, and a great concourse of people sitting in the body of the hall, waiting for the performance to begin. Presently the gas was turned down, and a man dressed in a smock frock, and straw hat and knee breeches, and carrying a long whip over his shoulders, came on the stage, and began to sing one of the devil's songs. I sat between my wife's uncle and the other gentleman; but the words, "What doest thou here?" found me out. I shouted at the top of my voice, "*The Lord save you all; but this is no place for a child of God, so I'll go.*" The man immediately left the stage, and I groped my way out into the sunshine.

THE SCEPTICAL DOCTOR.

At the close of the preaching one night, a gentleman put his card into my hand. On the back of the card I found written an invitation to his house in Cavendish Square. At supper that evening I handed the card to my host, and asked him if he knew the gentleman.

"Yes," he said; "he is a well-known doctor, a sceptic, and one of the greatest upholders of the theatre in London."

I was sorely troubled. I thought the sceptical doctor wanted me to go and argue with him, that he might have an opportunity of upsetting my belief. I was comforted by the assurance given in that word: "If any man lack wisdom, let him ask of God"; and I went to God for the promised wisdom.

When I got down to breakfast in the morning, I found a letter from the doctor, telling me to meet him if possible at eleven, and to take a cab at his expense. I did as desired; and when I got to the house was shown into a room the like of which I had never seen before: it was so beautiful. I was afraid to move, lest I should damage the carpet. By-and-by three young ladies came in, who told me they had been with the doctor at the meeting the night before, and had enjoyed it very much. Presently the doctor himself came in, and greeted me in a way that dispelled all my fears. He told me he had arranged matters so that he could have an hour or two with me; and he pressed me to stay and lunch with them. I agreed.

I knew I had no right to be there save as a worker for Christ; so I turned to one of the young ladies, and asked if Christ was hers. She said;

"No; but I wish He were!"

Putting a similar question to the others, I got from them a similar answer. Then I turned to my host, and asked him if Christ was precious to his soul.

He said, "No."

Then he went on to tell me he had had one of the best of mothers. He reminded me how, at the meeting on the previous evening, I had knelt on the platform with my hand on my head, and how I had said:

"Is there not some sinner here who had a praying mother? Her hand has been laid on your head in blessing. Perhaps your head is bald now; but you can never forget that mother's prayers."

The doctor told me that, while I was so speaking, conviction of sin had laid hold upon him. He remembered the days when he knelt in prayer at his mother's knee; he remembered the day when he stood by her dying bed, and she appealed to him to meet her in heaven. He confessed his desire to meet her above. It was with that object he had sent for me. He wanted me to tell him how I found peace. I told him how the Lord found me, and pardoned my sins. We knelt to pray. The ladies wept; the doctor wept; and He who wipes the tears from every eye came into that room and revealed Himself to those earnest seekers as their personal Saviour. I went to my lodgings rejoicing.

"AN HUNGERED," AND FED FROM HEAVEN.

Shortly after this I returned to Prescot for a little necessary rest. Many were under the impression that by leaving the coal-pit for the platform I had an eye to the bettering of my worldly condition. Had that been my motive, I would have been disappointed. It was so far otherwise, that soon after my return to my family there was no food in the house, nor was there any money to buy it. I remember one morning on which we had not broken our fast for thirty-six hours. I did not care for myself; but it was a severe trial to see my wife and two children foodless.

I had received an invitation to return to London; but I had no money to pay my fare. On the table were the tea-cups and other crockery; but there was nothing in the way of food. My wife sat with the baby on her knee. I took the Bible and read a portion of God's Word, and then knelt to pray. My little boy came to me and said:

"Stop praying, pa. Me *so* hungry. Give me my breakfast, and pray afterwards. Me so hungry."

He went to his mother, and said:

"Ma, I wish pa would stop praying, and give me my breakfast. Me so hungry."

He came again to me and laid his little face to mine. I felt his tears wet my cheek. I shall feel them to my dying day. What could I do but plead with God? There was a knock at the door. I got up from my knees and opened to the postman. He placed a registered letter in my hand. I signed the little paper and opened my letter. I found a five-pound note from an unknown friend. It meant food for my family and my fare to London.

I set off with my bag. When I reached Rainhill Station I found the parliamentary train had gone, so I had to take a second-class ticket. When I entered the compartment I was greeted with a social "Good morning!" by the gentleman who was already there. He immediately began to talk to me about politics. When I understood I replied; when I did not understand I held my peace. By-and-by I said to him:

"Let us change the subject."

He was willing, and asked what subject I wished to talk about.

I said, "God is love."

He dropped his paper and pulled off his hat, and said:

"Do you know anything of the love of God?"

"A little," I replied. "I know that He loves me and gave his Son for me."

He said, "Thank God!"

I suggested that we pray in the railway carriage. He agreed. I prayed, and he prayed, and I prayed again, and then I sang. When I had done singing, he asked my name.

"Richard Weaver," I said. In a moment his hand was thrust into his pocket for a well-filled purse, which he offered to me with the words:

"God bless you: this is yours."

"Nay," said I, "I cannot accept it until I know what it is for."

He asked if I remembered preaching in the theatre in Liverpool.

I said, "Yes."

"Well," he said, "I had a son who, through associating with bad companions, had become one of the worst characters in Liverpool. He was drinking and gambling to a fearful extent, and robbing us at home on every hand. He went to hear you preach, and came home a new man in Christ Jesus. He is now the greatest comfort we have got. This purse has been in my pocket for some time as a present to you for what the Lord, through you, has done for our boy."

I gratefully accepted the purse.

But the pleasant surprises of the day were yet to be added to. I was under promise to preach at Green Lane on my way to London. In order to keep that promise I broke my journey at Stafford, and got into the train for Wolverhampton. In the carriage were two navvies and a respectably dressed woman. As the train proceeded towards Wolverhampton, the navvies were talking with each other, and in their talk were frequently taking God's name in vain. At last I could bear it no longer; and I said to one of the men:

"Here, my good man, don't you call my Father names any more."

"Call your father names!" said he, "I never spoke a word about your father. I don't know him. Dost thee, Jim?"

"No," said his comrade.

"The more shame to you," said I. "If you knew my Father, you would love Him. So please don't call Him names any more."

I asked him to give me his hand. I spoke to him of God's love. He told me that six months before he had gone to see his dying mother, and she had put her hand on his head and asked God to bless him. He asked:

"Do you think, Sir, that God will save a sinner like me?"

We knelt in the carriage. The navvies cried to God, and their prayer was answered. One of those navvies is now a missionary of the Gospel.

When I got out at Wolverhampton, the woman who was in the carriage followed me, and asked if my name was Richard Weaver. She said she guessed it was, from my talk with the men. She went on to ask if I remembered preaching at such-and-such a place, some sixteen months before.

I said, "Yes."

She said, "The Lord bless thee! Sixteen months ago I had no bed but a bed of straw: my four children had nothing to eat. My husband had been put in prison, and had come out more like a devil than a man. As he came along he saw a placard with your name on it. He said to himself: 'That must be the man I used to work with in the coal-pit. I'll go and hear him.' Your text was, 'The Master is come, and calleth for thee.' He was the first to go to the penitent form.

"I was sitting at home that night in fear. When he came in there was only an inch of candle in the socket. He said, 'Where are the children?' 'Upstairs in bed,' I said. 'Bring them down,' said he. I laid the baby on the hearthstone and went upstairs, thinking he was about to turn us all out to seek shelter under some hedgerow. I knelt by my sleeping children, and asked the Lord to protect them; and then I awoke them and took them down. To my astonishment, my husband took the eldest into his arms and kissed her, and said, 'My dear lass, the Lord has sent thee a father home to-night.' He did the same with the second girl, and with the boy, and also with the baby. Then he put his arm around my neck, and kissed me, and said, 'My dear wife, the Lord has sent thee a husband home to-night.' Oh, Mr. Weaver, what a word! '*My dear wife.*' I had not heard it for fourteen years! How can I thank you? The Lord bless thee!"

Next morning there was a knock at the door of my room.

"Come in," I cried.

In walked four children, followed by a man, who said:

"God bless thee, Richard. I am the man that my wife told thee of yesterday."

There they stood, dressed in a way that showed at once respectability and comfort. We had a delightful thanksgiving meeting. In the strength of such encouragements I went on to London on the following day. I preached in the Surrey Theatre, the Victoria Theatre, the Borough Road Chapel, New Park Street Chapel, the Riding School in the West End, the City of London Theatre, Effingham Theatre, and other places. The Lord worked in a wonderful manner. Thieves were made honest; harlots were made virtuous; wives were reunited to their husbands, and husbands restored to their wives. Not a few who were known as "bad characters" were brought to Christ during that mission; and so thorough was the change and so complete the blotting out of their past, that they are known now only as devoted workers for Christ, some as evangelists and some as ministers, in different parts of the country. It was the Lord's doing. To Him be all the glory.

VIII.

In Scotland.

"I FEAR that you may not always be willing to lie still—you who have been like the Fiery Cross over hill and dale, gathering those to our Conqueror who are called and chosen faithful." (*Extract from letter written to Weaver by Mrs. Stewart Sandeman.*)

THE JOURNEY NORTH.

While labouring in London I received a telegram from Mr. Radcliffe, urging me to join him in Aberdeen. I made the arrangements necessary for the carrying on of the London work, and set off for the north country. I shall never forget that journey. I had overlooked the need of bodily sustenance. After we passed Carlisle, the pains of hunger took hold of me. It was then so late that all the refreshment rooms were closed. I had a bishop for a travelling companion. He had abundance of the good things of this life, and there he sat eating and drinking, and keeping me yearning for an invitation to partake with him. I reached Aberdeen without receiving the invitation so urgently wished for. I thought the bishop lacking in compassion; but it is probable that it never occurred to him that I must be hungry.

Campaign Begins at Perth.

On reaching the address from which Mr. Radcliffe wired me, I was astonished at noticing that the servant-girl who opened the door wore neither shoes nor stockings. Better acquaintance with the customs of the Aberdonians let me know that it was no uncommon thing for the servants in the summer-time to do their work barefooted. On asking for Mr. Radcliffe, I was told he had gone to Perth the day before. On giving my name, however, a hearty welcome was accorded me. I telegraphed to Perth, and got a reply from Mr. Radcliffe asking me to join him there. I returned to Perth that same day, and in that city Mr. Radcliffe and I laboured for some time. Blessed results followed the preaching of the word.

En Route to Glasgow.

Leaving Perth on our way to Glasgow, we travelled by means of a horse and carriage, and preached at the various towns and villages we passed through. At Crieff, a platform had been erected in a field, and thousands had assembled to hear the word. When I had done speaking, I invited the anxious to follow Mr. Radcliffe and myself to the other side of the field. To our surprise, hundreds followed us to ask, "What must we do to be saved?" We heard of whole families being kept awake all night with joy that salvation had visited their homes.

At Braco we had a similar meeting about four in the afternoon. As we had to hurry on to Stirling, we left the anxious ones in the hands of the ministers and Christian workers of the district.

In Stirling we held a meeting in the Corn Exchange. The meeting lasted all night. Far on in the morning I retired to the hotel for a little rest; but about five o'clock the "boots" of the hotel called me up, and told me Mr. Radcliffe wanted me to return to the Exchange to sing to those still there. I found there were yet between thirty and forty inquiring the way of salvation. As I went in I met a working man and his wife on their way out. I asked him if he had found Christ. He said:

"No; but I can stay no longer. I have to go to my work."

I took hold of their hands, saying:

"I will sing just one verse. The Lord help you to make it yours." I sang:

> Just as I am, without one plea,
> But that thy blood was shed for me,
> And that Thou bid'st me come to Thee:
> O Lamb of God, I come.

The man said, "It is done! Christ is mine!" The woman also believed. They embraced each other, and went home rejoicing in God their Saviour.

On Glasgow Green.

We reached Glasgow on the following day. We had been advertised to preach on Glasgow Green. A large platform had been erected. A Glasgow gentleman presided. Each speaker was allowed ten minutes. As soon as the ten minutes were up the chairman rang a bell. When my turn came, I looked at the vast concourse of people, and said:

"I will sing first." I sang:

> In evil long I took delight,
>   Unawed by shame or fear,
> Till a new object met my sight,
>   And stopped my wild career.
>
>   Oh, the Lamb, the bleeding Lamb,
>   The Lamb upon Calvary;
>   The Lamb that was slain, that liveth again,
>   To intercede for me.

As I sang, I heard the ministers on the platform saying:

"This might do for England, but it will never do for Scotland."

Before the hymn was finished the people had joined in the chorus. I began to speak. The Lord was with me. The bell was rung for me to stop. I turned round and said:

"Thee can ring the bell, but I'm not going to stop."

I went on preaching. The Spirit came in such power that many were struck down under the word, and had to be carried into a neighbouring church. There they lay on the floor as if dead. For a time they seemed to be unconscious of everything around them.

THE HOME DOOR NEVER BARRED.

One poor girl was laid on the floor of the church. A doctor felt her pulse and said, "She is not dead." By-and-by she sat up and said, "Christ for me!" Her home was a little cot on the side of a hill in a glen near Blair Athole. Nine years had passed since she left her mother's protecting care. Pardoned by God, she started at once for her old home. She begged by day, and travelled by night. Barefooted, sorefooted, and weary, she toiled on in the storm, supported, as she told me afterwards, by the thought of reaching her mother. It was late at night when she reached the glen. A light shone through the window of the little cot on the hillside. She reached the door and knocked. There was no answer. The old widowed mother lay in the box-bed, as they call it; but she knew not what to make of the knock at that hour of the night.

The girl outside trembled with cold, and knocked again and again: still there was no answer. At last she put her hand upon the latch, and lifted it, and the door at once opened. Then the mother cried:

"Who's there?"

"It's me, mother," said the weary daughter.

The mother sprang out of bed, turned up the light, that she might see her daughter better; clasped her in a warm and loving embrace; took off her wet things, and put on dry; and seated her at the little table, on which soon appeared a warm and refreshing supper. By-and-by the daughter said:

"Mother, how is it that the door was not locked to-night?"

"My dear child," said the mother, "that door has never been locked since you left nine years ago. I thought you would return home to your mother, and I left it unbarred for you."

How like our Heavenly Father!

A PUBLICAN PREFERRING CHRIST TO CUSTOMERS.

After working for some time in Glasgow we went to Greenock, and there held open-air meetings. The district was moved for miles around. *It seemed at that time as if the Millennium were at hand.* From

Greenock we went to Saltcoats, and thence to Ardrossan. Again the Lord worked wondrously. Let me give you one case from that neighbourhood. My favourite hymn at that time was that which begins:

> My heart is fixed, eternal God,
>   Fixed on Thee! fixed on Thee!
> And my immortal choice is made:
>   Christ for me! Christ for me!

The wife and daughter of a Dunlop publican had come to the meetings at Ardrossan. They went home to Dunlop new creatures in Christ Jesus. They began to sing, "Christ for me!" It was carried home by the power of God's Spirit to the heart of the publican, and he fell on the floor as if dead. When he became conscious, the first words he was heard to utter were, "Christ for me!" Young men were sent to pull down his sign, and he declared what the Lord had done for his soul. When the other publican heard, he swaggeringly said:

"Yes, it is Christ for him, and all the customers for me."

But the work of the Spirit broke out in full force in the place. One night a band of young men and women passed his place singing a gospel hymn. He thought he would like to hear what they were singing; so he came and stood in his doorway. It was the hymn, "Christ for me!" The arrow reached his heart. He fell on his knees crying, "What must I do to be saved?" The Lord pardoned his sins, and he too had his sign taken down; and I am told that for a time Dunlop was without a public-house. *The Gospel of regeneration is the best Temperance lecture I know.*

In the Calton Jail, Edinburgh.

After a brief sojourn in the South, I returned North, to hold meetings in Edinburgh. While there I was asked to preach in Calton Jail. I spoke first in the women's ward. As I looked at the eighty gathered to hear me I felt they had had plenty of harsh words; so I spoke of the love of God, and I sang, "Rest for the weary." Those who desired to have conversation with me were asked to put out their numbers. In this way I had the privilege of dealing with upwards of thirty anxious inquirers.

As I was about to leave the prison, the kind-hearted governor pointed to one of the cells, and said:

"In that cell is the worst character in all the prison; I have put her on low diet and in chains, but I cannot break her will. She has not put out her number; but I wish you would pay her a visit also."

The cell door was opened. On the three-legged stool in the centre of her cell sat the wretched inmate. Putting my hand on her shoulder, I said:

"God bless you! The Lord loves you."

"No, He doesn't," was her reply. "I am too bad for God to love."

"But," I said, "God commendeth his love toward us, in that while we were yet sinners, Christ died for us."

After some further conversation, she dropped on her knees and uttered the cry:

"Thank God, some one loves me!"

I prayed with her, and left the cell. Next day, as I was preaching in another part of the prison, a letter was put into my hand, with the request that it be read to the other women. It was from the woman of whom I have spoken, and it was to testify that the Lord had pardoned her sins. As soon as I had read out the name of the writer, several cried out:

"If God can save her, He can save me."

Several put out their numbers as a sign that they wanted to be spoken to; and I went from cell to cell to tell of the salvation that is in Jesus. The stories they told of the way in which they had been entangled into sin and crime were so heartrending that I left the prison humbled at the remembrance that it was only through the grace of God that my lot was different from theirs.

WHEN THE FINE IS PAID THE PRISONER IS FREE.

A few days later Mr. Radcliffe and I went again to the prison; this time to speak to the men. The power of God was on the meeting. The usual invitation to put out the number was given. In going round the cells of those who had done so, we came to a cell in which we found the inmate on his knees. I asked him if he wanted Christ.

"No," he replied.

I asked, "What are you praying for, then?"

He said, "For my wife and children."

He went on to tell us that the Lord had already found him in the meeting, and had pardoned his sins. I asked his wife's address, giving as my reason that I meant to go and tell her how the Lord had had mercy on her husband.

"God bless you," he said. "Tell her to cheer up, as I come out of prison a new man in Christ Jesus; and if God spare us, there are happier days in store for her and the children."

We left him praising God. By-and-by Mr. Radcliffe asked the Governor what this man was in for.

"Drunk and disorderly," was the answer.

"What is the amount of his fine?"

"Ten shillings."

Mr. Radcliffe paid the fine, and the prisoner was free. As he shook hands with the turnkey, he said: "By the grace of God, you will not catch me here again."

I preached that evening in St. John's Church, and in the inquiry meeting found the man who had been liberated from the prison in the morning. He pleaded with me to go and speak with a companion he had brought to the meeting. I found that his companion was one of those who imagine they have to wait awhile and get better before they come to Christ. Turning to my friend, I said:

"Tell your friend what you had to do to get out of prison after your fine was paid." He turned round to his weeping companion, and said:

"Look here, I was in prison this morning, and my penalty was fourteen days or ten shillings. Now, I hadn't ten pence; and if I had knelt down and prayed, that wouldn't have paid my fine. If I had wept, that would not have given me liberty. Mr. Radcliffe went and paid my fine. What he did for me satisfied the law, and opened my cell door, and told me to walk out."

"That's it," said I. "When Christ died on the cross, He paid the sinner's fine. He satisfied Divine justice: He met the Law's demands; and He tells you, by believing, to walk out of your sins."

Then the poor man said: "*It is not, then, what Christ will do?*"

"*No*," I said, "*it is what Christ has done.*"

He jumped up, seized my hand, and said: "I believe; and I walk out of my sins into the liberty wherewith Christ maketh his people free."

In the Queen's Park.

One Sabbath evening I was advertised to preach in the Queen's Park. The platform belonging to the garrison, and on which the band played, had been secured for the occasion, and erected at a suitable place. As I took my stand on it, I found myself in an amphitheatre made by the Lord. Some estimated the crowd at forty thousand. It was so great that I was afraid that I could not make myself heard by all. I got some friends to go to the outskirts of the crowd on the upper part of the hill and hold up their hands if they heard and understood.

Having in this way discovered that my voice was carrying, I preached from those words of Elijah: "How long halt ye between two opinions?" I look on that service as one of the most wonderful in all my experience. I felt that the God of Elijah was with me. We held the meeting for inquirers in the Assembly Hall. The number of those who with broken heart were seeking Christ was very great. One of them had a sad tale to tell me. Drawing from beneath her cloak a rope, she said:

"Take this, sir. I was on my way to drown myself, and this rope was to tie my legs. I heard the sound of singing in the park. I turned aside to see whence it came, and was thus led to your meeting. Your singing of 'Christ for me!' was the means of opening my eyes. Instead of being drowned, and condemned, I am now in this hall saved, and having life in Christ, my risen Lord. How can I praise Him for what He has done for me!"

DUNCAN MATHESON ON RICHARD WEAVER.

The following extracts from letters written by the late Duncan Matheson give his impressions of Weaver. They refer to this period.

Speaking of his preaching, Matheson wrote:

His appeals were overwhelming. I have seldom seen such an impression produced on a people. It seemed an hour of solemn decision. The hall was still as the grave and solemn as eternity itself. It is evident God gave the word to various classes of sinners with convincing power.

Speaking of his attractive personality, and alluding to Peden's sigh at Richard Cameron's grave, he wrote:

When he goes home, not a few of us will say, "Oh to be wi' Ritchie!"

The following extracts from letters written by Weaver himself tell their own tale.

HOSTILITY FROM THE PUBLIC-HOUSE.

One week I was at ——, and Satan seemed to be let loose upon me. He called a meeting of his faithful followers. He drew attention to what he had done for the place; how he had built two hundred houses to make sober men drunkards, and good husbands bad husbands; to ruin bodies and fill prisons. He pointed to the way in which the preaching of the Gospel was interfering with his dominion. He urged them to be up and doing, to make the town safe as before. To this end he urged them to tell as many lies as they could, and get drunk as often as they could; and they would have his reward. So he exhorted, and his followers obeyed; but in spite of it all, it seems that Scotland's harvest day has come.

In another letter we have evidence that Weaver paid considerable attention to our Lord's command to "BE WISE AS SERPENTS." He writes as follows:—

I find it more my duty every day not to prejudice the people against me; but to seek to win them over by love, and then I have a chance of preaching Jesus to them. I am sorry to see in the last number of *The Revival* my name mentioned in connection with the preaching of two ladies with whom I am in no way connected. It is calculated to do me harm, by shutting doors which I believe the Lord has opened and is opening to me in Scotland. I am not going to condemn nor justify the preaching of women; but we know that in Scotland it is almost universally condemned. It is our duty not to stir up the people to anger, but to remember it is written, "As much as lieth in you, live peaceably with all men."

That description of how it was in the sixties is exceedingly interesting to one who reads it with knowledge of how it is in the nineties. We have come far since the days of which Weaver wrote. Opinions change, even in Scotland.

In another letter Weaver cries:

"BACK TO THE CROSS!"

He says:—

The Revival is on the decline only where labourers are taking their minds off the Cross. I have watched with pain how they have left the Cross, and have taken up with other things. Paul's cry was, "God forbid that I should glory, save in the Cross of our Lord Jesus Christ." Look at sinners how they are flocking to hell. Let us take our stand between them and the pit, and do our utmost to stop their headlong rush.

In another we have this resolution:—

I have made a covenant with the Lord this year to be a greater fool for Christ and his cause than ever. Souls are going down to death and hell by thousands. If one method fails, I must try others.

Another letter reveals *the white heat* of his soul. It closes thus:

Pray, pray; believe, believe; Christ, Christ; blood, blood—for sinners.

Ever yours in Christ,
RICHARD WEAVER.

Closing Soirée in City Hall, Glasgow.

A four weeks' mission in Glasgow was brought to a close by a Soirée in the City Hall. Some 2,400 were present. The Lord Provost occupied the chair, and in the course of his address said that magistrates were meant to be a terror to evil-doers and a praise to them that do well. He lamented the amount of their time taken up with the former, as compared with the time they were able to devote to the latter. He affirmed that it was in the latter capacity he was present that evening, and he said the change was to him one that was exceeding pleasant.

In the course of an address given by Mr. (now Dr.) Wells occurs this testimony: "I have met with some Christians who think good has been done, but that there have been some extravagances. I have attended Revival meetings for the last six years, and have never seen any in which there was so little to be regretted. I have become personally acquainted with twelve men and their wives and families who never used to attend any place of worship, but are now concerned about their souls, if not actually decided to be on the Lord's side."

Mr. Howie read a letter that Mr. Weaver had received. In the course of the letter the writer said: "You have, under God, rescued me from the dark cavern of Atheism—from the gloom, the peril, the wretchedness of that revolting system. I have wandered far in search of God, ransacked the works of heathen sages and Christian writers, without a ray of light. I have listened to the teachings of Holyoake, Iconoclast, and others, which only drove me further into the labyrinth of doubt, impiety, and despair. The blessed truth that 'the Lord God omnipotent reigneth' now shines in my mind. I have received the clearest evidence of his power and goodness towards me. Praise the Lord, and magnify his name, for directing my steps to the City Hall to hear you expound and illustrate the soul-saving truths of the Gospel of Christ."

The Rev. Jas. Gall, of the Moray Free Church, Edinburgh, said that no one had stirred that city to its depths as Weaver had done; and nobody had been so blessed in bringing souls to the Saviour. There was no hall in Edinburgh like the one in which they were met; but there was the Queen's Park, where between twenty and thirty thousand had gathered to hear the Word of God from Weaver's lips: and not only were multitudes of souls immediately brought to Christ, but the brethren of Carrubbers Close Mission had been engaged for weeks after he had gone, in gathering in the fruits of his labours.

In the Free Church Cathedral.

A correspondent thus describes a service conducted by Weaver in Free St. George's, Edinburgh:

His prayer was one of those appeals of felt infirmity, which draws every believing heart along with it close up to the footstool of the King, and makes you feel that it is impossible the blessing should not come. His text was, "God so loved the world," etc. He showed us that all apprehensions or discoveries of the measure of God's love made as yet, in confessions, standards, or individual believers' experiences, were true and real approaches to the knowledge of it; but left its mainsprings, depths, and boundaries, extending far beyond the limits of our knowledge.

He closed with this original illustration:

When a boy, I one day went bathing with another boy who was playing truant from school. He had some chalk in his pocket, and after our bath he proposed that we should climb to the top of the Shropshire hill, at the foot of which flowed the stream in which we had bathed. With his chalk he was to write our names on the blue heavens that seemed to us to rest on that hill-top. We reached the summit to meet with a great astonishment. The blue sky was as far above us as ever. Have you a mind to find out how far God's love to ruined man can stretch? Do you think you can write its limits down? Just try and climb one height that you suppose to measure it; and up there on the blue heavens of his compassions write how much God loves the world. You'll find the task impossible. You'll be compelled to give up the attempt, and fall back on this: "God so loved the world, that He gave his only-begotten Son." When you can tell the full glory of that gift, then, and only then, will you be able to fathom the depths of that " so."

Every king of men has his poet laureate, and Weaver was not without his. At the farewell meeting in Edinburgh a leaflet of original verses by Mr. R. Meek was distributed. The strain of the verses may be gathered from the following selection:

> What mighty gathering's yon,
> 'Midst blaze of light and architecture grand!
> It awes the soul such crowd to look upon,
> At once a solemn and a happy band.
>
> A brilliant throng we see,
> Both working folks and noble ladies fair,
> All full of joy, a loving family,
> With good Professor Simpson in the chair.

K

In Scotland.

All met to honour him,
The dauntless Richard Weaver, rough and plain,
Yet true and zealous for Jehovah's name—
Nor wise that man who would his work disdain.

What eloquence divine
Flowed from his lips in pleading with the soul
Estranged from God, and taken up with wine,
That each would now his wickedness control!

Yes, Scotland, thou hast been
Allowed once more another star to see
Shining amidst the darkness—yet unseen
By all who will not with the truth agree.

IX.

In Ireland, Wales, and Dreamland.

A Time to Pray, and a Time to Trust.

WE had an exceedingly rough passage when I went to preach in Dublin; but I knew that my Father held the winds in his fists and the sea in the hollow of his hand; and that knowledge kept me from being afraid. The vessel rolled and plunged dreadfully; and as I lay in my berth I began to feel very uncomfortable.

In a berth near mine lay an aged Catholic priest. His fears drove him to prayer. At last I shouted:

"Stop praying, man; this is not the time to pray." In a tone of surprise he said:

"What! I think this is the very time to pray."

"Not at all, man," said I. "I prayed at Holyhead when I was on land, and I *trust* the Lord now. This is the time to TRUST."

"Hear, hear!" said the other passengers; and we heard the prayers of the priest no more.

In the Metropolitan Hall, Dublin.

An esteemed correspondent has furnished the following account of his first meeting:

I recollect Richard Weaver's first appearance in Dublin. Whether it was in '59 or '60 I cannot say. It was during our time of Revival in Ireland. The first time he spoke his text was: "How wilt thou do in the swellings of Jordan?" He came into the Metropolitan Hall immediately after landing at the North Wall, and without waiting for refreshments. The hall was crowded; in some parts there was scarcely standing room. His powerful voice filled the building; and, as he spoke, telling us in thrilling words the story of his life and conversion, a pin-fall could have been heard, so intense was the stillness. He swayed that vast multitude as one man. I do not remember much of the sermon, as it is nearly forty years ago; but the text, "How wilt thou do in the swellings of Jordan?" impressed me greatly. As he paced up and down the platform, repeating it again and again, it just seemed as if there was a compelling power behind the words; so touching men's hearts that they had to bow to an unseen, but felt Presence. I can never forget the preacher and his text. I was a Christian already; but he did me good. All through his stay with us he drew great crowds. "The memory of the just is blessed."

EMILY HALLIDAY.

We resume the personal narrative.

NEITHER A CATHOLIC NOR A PROTESTANT.

A day or two after my arrival in Dublin, a young gentleman friend took me a drive through Phœnix Park in a jaunting car. I said to our driver:

"Jarvy, have you been to hear that man preach?"

"What man, your honour?"

"A man from England. He is called 'The Converted Collier.' He preaches in the Metropolitan Hall."

"Ah, sure enough, your honour, I'm a Catholic."

"Well, Jarvy, he is neither a Catholic nor a Protestant. I am going to the Hall to-night; and if you go I'll give you a shilling."

"Ah, sure enough, I will go then."

"Well, you will see me there, and you must come to me for your shilling."

"I will, your honour."

Night came, and when I arrived at the Hall there was a crowded congregation. As I stood on the platform I espied my Jarvy, with three others up in the gallery to my right hand. As I gave out the hymn and began to sing "Christ for me!" I could hear him say to his friends, "Ah, sure enough, that's the gentleman that rode with me." I sang and prayed and preached, and the presence of Christ was there to kill and make alive.

After I had gone into the ante-room who should walk in but the Jarvy. I thought he had come for his shilling; so I pulled one out, and handing it to him, said:

"Here is your shilling."

"Ah, sure, sir," he said, "I will not have it. I came in here a Catholic, but I go out neither Catholic nor Protestant. It is now 'Christ for me!'"

Years afterwards I met that man, and his song was still the same.

Do you Think Christ has Done it All?

While preaching in Limerick, I was invited one afternoon to dine with a gentleman who lived in the neighbourhood. On our way to his house, we saw a poor woman on her knees, making towards a cross some forty yards distant. As she went painfully along the gravel, she was counting her beads. I thought I should like to go and speak to her, but my friend said, "You must not do it; they will murder you." I prayed to God to open the poor woman's eyes.

A Roman Catholic woman, who had been converted, got this woman to come and hear me preach in the evening. My text was: "God so loved the world," etc.

As soon as I had done, the poor woman who had been doing penance came and asked if I thought the Lord had done it all.

"To be sure He has," said I.

Before the week was finished, Christ was the "*all and in all*" of that woman's salvation.

CHEYNE BRADY ON WEAVER'S WORK IN IRELAND.

Richard Weaver was a faithful preacher of the Gospel—one of the Lord's "mighty men." When he preached at Merrion Hall, Dublin, the place was crowded. There he stood on the platform, giving out a hymn. Often he introduced a new one to the congregation. First, he sang the hymn by himself, and then gave out two lines at a time, and went over and over again until they knew it. I remember when he slowly taught the vast assembly to sing

> Nothing, either great or small,
> Nothing, sinner, no ;
> Jesus did it, did it all,
> Long, long ago.

Patiently he taught the words and music to the audience, and made them repeat it until they knew it, and the vast throng shouted the refrain :

> It is finished, yes, indeed,
> Finished, every jot :
> Sinner, this is all you need,
> Tell me, is it not ?

By this time the meeting was thrilled and in touch with the preacher, and ready to hear the proclamation of God's love in sending the Lord Jesus to die for our sins.

The love of Jesus was a favourite theme. He impressed the truth oftentimes with hymn-singing. How efficacious was his singing of

> Jesus loves me, this I know,
> For the Bible tells me so.

or of

> My heart is fixed, eternal God,
> Fixed on Thee! fixed on Thee.

with the ringing chorus,

> Christ for me, Christ for me.

or of

> Oh, happy day, that fixed my choice
> On Thee, my Saviour and my God.

A notice of Richard Weaver's work in Ireland would be incomplete without reference to our beloved and lamented friend, Henry Bewley, who witnessed for Christ for many years, and gave largely of his substance, by building Merrion Hall, printing numerous tracts, supporting the evangelists, &c. He delighted to encourage Richard Weaver, and esteemed him highly.

Under Weaver's preaching, men and women of all classes were broken down. It was noticed of him that he spent much time in reading and prayer in his room in the home of the hospitable William Fry, whose house was open at all times to the many evangelists who visited Dublin.

Weaver was of very simple habits. Though run after by titled ladies, he was not spoiled. Children loved him; his conduct in the family circle was most winning with the young. His work was stamped with the approval of his Divine Master, and the poor heard him gladly.

His memory is cherished in Dublin, where many to this day attribute their conversion to his faithful preaching of the Gospel of the Lord Jesus Christ.

Weaver was a model evangelist; his beaming countenance declared his faith. His face shone with the love of God. His daily life was consistent; he preached the truth not only in word, but in act.

He was a Christ-man.

CHEYNE BRADY.

JOSEPH ACTON ON THE WORK.

Dublin, May 3, 1895.

Mr. RICHARD WEAVER,

Beloved Brother in Christ,

Seeing your address in this week's issue of *The Christian*, I thought I should drop you a line, as it brought to my mind the blessed times we had many years ago in Dublin, when the Lord was using his Word preached by you to the salvation of hundreds of precious souls. And the awakened were not a few, who afterwards were brought to trust Christ as the Saviour of the lost, and are standing monuments to-day of God's keeping power as well as saving grace.

In Cardiff.

I went to Cardiff on receipt of an invitation signed by some hundreds of those who were interested in the work of the Lord. There, as at other places, the Lord did marvellous things. Time would fail me to describe the cases that came under my own personal notice and the notice of my friends. Some of all classes were brought to Christ. On the last Sabbath of my stay I was to preach three times in the Circus.

On the Saturday evening I told the people that we would turn out at six on the Sabbath morning, and mission the streets. So the next morning I went at the time appointed. Some five or six thousand were waiting to go with me. What a sight it was! Well, we missioned the streets. In one street of ill-fame I divided the people, and walked down the midst of them, giving a warning voice to people that were still in bed. Windows were thrown up. Poor fallen sisters and sinful brothers came to listen. I reminded them of the Judgment to come. Tears stole down many a cheek. Some were seen in their houses wringing their hands and crying for mercy.

As I was proclaiming salvation to those lost and ruined children of Adam, I overstrained my voice, broke a blood-vessel, and fell backwards into the arms of a friend who was following me with my coat. Blood was flowing out of my mouth. I had to stop speaking in the open air. By the help of the Lord I was enabled to preach three times as promised in the Circus. I was in great weakness: but the Lord was there in power; and many were those who found Him. Broken down in health, I left Cardiff and went home to Cheshire.

"He won't Take what the Doctor Orders."

I became so weak through ill-health that I could not walk, nor even feed myself. But the Lord was precious. The doctor held out no hope of my recovery; but my prospects were bright, for whether living or dying I was the Lord's. One day, when the doctor came he ordered alcoholic stimulants. I said:

"No, doctor; I haven't tasted that for years, and I'm not going to. Even if it be death, Christ is mine, and heaven is my home."

He said, "Well, Mr. Weaver, all I can say is, you are very stupid. I come here in the name of the Lord, to give you my advice, and for the sake of Christ's cause I try to do you good; but if you will not take what I order, I can do no good by visiting you, and I shall not come again."

He told my wife I was so self-willed that he would not come again. After he had gone, my wife sat on one side of the fireplace and I on the other, with our little son between us. She was silently weeping. Our child looking up saw his mother's tears, and asked:

"What are you weeping for, ma?"

She said, "Because your father wants to leave us. He won't take what the doctor orders. He wants you to be without a father, and me without a husband."

He got up on my knee, and said, "You *don't* want

to go to heaven, and leave ma and me, *do* you, pa? You *will* do what the doctor tells you, won't you?"

The child's words and look went to my heart. I was helped to bed. I was left alone. There I lay with the child's words and look on my mind. By-and-by I fell asleep, and had a strange dream.

"YOU HAVE COME TO HEAVEN BEFORE YOUR TIME."

I dreamt I was dead, and that my death had occurred at the same time as the death of my two dearest friends, Mr. Bewley and Mr. Fry. We were clothed in the white raiment spoken of in the Word. Arm-in-arm with each other, we were making our way up a beautiful street. Looking towards the earth, we saw the people attending our funerals. One of the most glorious Beings that ever eyes beheld came to meet us. Addressing Mr. Bewley, He asked, "How came you in here?" "Through the blood of the Lamb," was Mr. Bewley's answer. Unseen singers struck up the chorus, "Worthy is the Lamb." When the singing paused, Mr. Bewley was invited to enter into the joy of his Lord. He disappeared from our view.

Mr. Fry was next taken away in a similar manner, and I was left alone. I thought the countenance of the glorious One changed as He asked, "Richard Weaver, how came you in here?" I tremblingly said: "Through the blood of the Lamb." He said, "Come with Me." He took me where we could see a dreadful precipice; it was the precipice of hell. As I stood gazing I could see men and women with bandages over their eyes groping and stumbling towards this precipice. Ever and anon with a shriek and a cry for help, some poor blindfolded stumbler fell headlong into the abyss.

My Guide turned to me and solemnly said: "Richard Weaver, you have come to heaven before your time. I want you to go back to earth, and do what you can to pull the bandages from the eyes of those whom I have redeemed with my own blood." I said, "Lord, I am willing."

I awoke, and behold! it was a dream. But from the dream I believed that God was going to restore me to such health as would permit me to serve Him yet a little while longer on earth; and I was raised from that bed of weakness and permitted to climb back to the sunny heights of health. And unto me it has been given to be instrumental, in the hands of the Saviour of men, in removing the bandages of sin and degradation from the eyes of hundreds—yea, I may say, thousands—some of whom are walking in the light in the towns up and down England, some in Scotland, some in Ireland, and some in Wales. It is the doing of the Lord alone. To Him be all the praise!

"Your Money Perish with You."

It is characteristic of Weaver that in his own story of his life is no mention of his refusal of what some would call a "magnificent offer" from America. In the year 1868, two gentlemen from the United States sought a personal interview with him in order to secure a promise from him to go to the States on a preaching tour. Unfortunately they came not with the appeal: "Come over and help us," but with the temptation: "Come, and we'll give you —— thousand dollars and pay all your expenses."

It only made Weaver certain that it was not a call from God. Like the Hebrew youths, he was "not careful" to give his answer. The men with whom the dollar is a power were greatly astonished at his blunt reply:

"Your money perish with you: I shall not go." It needed a bigger attraction than the prospect of netting dollars to draw Weaver across the Atlantic.

A Thank-Offering Returned.

Nor is there mention of his return of a munificent thank-offering. At the close of a successful mission in C——, Weaver was surprised with the gift of the title deeds of two villas in the neighbourhood. Taken unawares, Weaver accepted the "deeds." But he could not sleep. He believed that his acceptance of the gift would afford the enemy a handle, and interfere with his success in winning souls, should he have the privilege of returning to that neighbourhood. He felt he had not the smile of God on what he had done. Fearing to allow the temptation to be dallied with longer, he got up between two and three in the morning, went and rung up the minister who had invited him to the town, and asked:

"Mr. ——, do you ever wish me to return to this town?"

"Why, certainly," said the minister.

"Then take back those title deeds," said Weaver, and he flung them at the minister's feet and hurried off before a word of protest could be uttered in reply.

X.

Holding the Fort at Hollinwood.

IN the life-story that I have been tracing, it has hitherto been a case of keeping company with a pilgrim whose pathway was flooded in sunshine. He has proved his Saviour's worth in the day of prosperity: he is now to have an opportunity of discovering His priceless value in the night of adversity. Experiences lie before him, such as those the Psalmist describes in the words: "They laid to my charge things that I knew not: they rewarded me evil for good to the spoiling of my soul" (Psalm xxxv. 11, 12).

For the sake of readers who have not the opportunity that I have had, I would say that careful and full investigation of all that can be learned regarding Weaver's trial, in the district in which it occurred, completely swept away from my own mind every vestige of suspicion of Richard's innocence. For the five and twenty years of his life that remained he constantly affirmed it, and when he lay on his deathbed, with full consciousness that he was about to depart, he reiterated, of his own accord, the solemn assertion that the dart that had wounded him was the poisoned arrow of a groundless calumny.

I lately asked the neighbours if Mr. Weaver had as

great power of drawing an audience after he passed under the cloud as he had before, and they told me that in that respect it made not the slightest difference. "You had only to put a waggon into the corner of a field—it mattered not where—and let it be known that Weaver was to preach, and at the hour the people were there in thousands!" This was the graphic way in which a Cheshire farmer put it. I was told that no one that ever visited the district got the audience that gathered to hear Richard Weaver.

Nor may I omit a seemingly trifling, but in this direction very significant incident of which I myself had personal cognizance. I spent the Christmas of 1896 at Moss Bank, the home in which Weaver breathed his last, and in which the bereaved members of his household still reside. It is a modest villa in the Cheshire village that is famous for the large number of its castellated homes of Manchester merchant princes. How those mansions are crowded on the foliage-covered slopes of Alderley Edge! The "waits" of the district, who on Christmas Eve carried round the echoes of the song sung by the angels to the shepherds of Bethlehem on the Advent that cut the history of the world in twain, did not forget the humble home of the family of the late veteran evangelist. No fewer than four bands came to pay their respects to the memory of Richard Weaver. At the castles of the wealthy the sacred serenade might be a means of procuring a contribution. At Moss Bank it was purely an expression of gratitude and of affection and of esteem.

The following letter from an English Church vicar refers to this period. It is the spontaneous testimony of one who writes with local knowledge of Weaver's trial.

Bempton Vicarage, Yorkshire,
Feby. 2, 1897.

My Dear Sir,—When I was curate of Chorley, Alderley Edge, in 1863-5, I had the great pleasure of making the acquaintance of the redoubtable Richard Weaver. On more than one occasion, when engaged in the afternoon service in our beautiful church, did I hear Richard's mighty and pathetic voice rolling across the village from the tent in which large numbers of people were hanging on his words.

Richard called on me, and I could see that he was fully grounded in and apprehended by Christ, *no more to go out.* A sterling God's man, his preaching of repentance towards God, and faith towards our Lord Jesus Christ, was ever telling and tender—never putting asunder what God has joined together.

In 1870 I heard him deliver a very Scriptural and searching discourse in the chapel of the immense Sunday School edifice in Macclesfield, where many were bowed down. There was no attempt to get up a Revival or sensational effect, a course ever, to my mind, derogatory to the presence, promise, and purpose of the Divine and Sovereign Spirit of the Saviour.

Yes, poor Weaver passed through the fire and the water; but God brought him out.

Gladly contributing these few lines,
Believe me, dear Sir, faithfully yours,
Nicholas McGrath.

Towards the close of the year 1872, the proprietors of *The Christian* received an account of special services, conducted by Weaver, in the Free Gospel Hall, Leicester. Desiring to be assured that the glowing account was not exaggerated, they paid a visit to the town, and witnessed for themselves the remarkable work in progress. The report read as follows:—

We have had brother Richard Weaver for some four weeks or so, holding revival meetings in the Free Gospel Hall, Leicester.

I have in bygone days been at many meetings where Richard has been preaching, but never at any of these meetings have I witnessed the power of an Almighty arm made more visibly bare than I have witnessed at very many of these meetings; nor have I ever heard Weaver speak with more of the Spirit's power than of late; and I am quite sure, from what I have heard from others who have been ten, twenty, and up to forty years, preachers, that they, like myself, have never experienced more of the divine presence in the soul since the days of their first stepping into the glorious liberty of the sons of God; and never have I seen more clear conversions to God than I have witnessed in the Gospel Hall. Dead souls have been quickened, backsliders have been reclaimed, and believers have rejoiced that God has been speaking in, through, and by his servant, with such a power that has not been often felt in Leicester; and eternity only can reveal the good that is going on at the Gospel Hall. I do not just speak individually, for hundreds would tell much more than I have here related. Brethren, pray for him, that the Lord will still use him to his glory, and give him strength of body, as well as soul. He requires our prayers. He had a very bad fit on Saturday night, which is the second since he came to Leicester. Nevertheless, he preached twice on the following day, when at the prayer-meeting a great many anxious souls came to the penitent forms to get a touch of Jesus as He was passing by.—I remain, your humble servant,

W. J. Mayor.

Weaver's own account of the days of darkness that he passed through is as follows:

"Every heart knows its own sorrow, and every back its own burden"; but I have sometimes thought that no man has ever had the troubles that I have had to contend with. Afflictions sore have been my lot.

I have had physical weakness to battle against. Ever since the time of my dream I have been obliged to walk with a stick to steady myself. For years I was troubled with epileptic fits. At times it required as many as five men to hold me. At other times I have been unconscious for hours together.

I have had poverty and want to endure. I have seen wife and children weeping for lack of the food that I, as bread-winner, had failed to procure.

But the greatest trial of all was when things that I knew not were laid to my charge. It is reported of Wesley that on one occasion, when preaching in a Dublin pulpit, he said that every sin had been laid to his charge save one; and he went on to say, "When I am charged with that also my crown will be found." In that respect I can shake hands with the venerable founder of the Wesleyan Church. I have never yet been counted a thief; but every other sin has been laid at my door.

To add to the bitterness, I was forsaken by many of my earthly friends. Some of those who had been the most profuse in their professions of attachment to me were the readiest to "drop" me.

Thus, I have had trials and temptations of various kinds, and from different sources. But not one trial too many; not one affliction too severe; not one temptation too strong. I was never allowed to lose my confidence in God. He who said to Peter, "I have prayed for thee, that thy faith fail not," must have been interceding for me. He also graciously allowed me to know, in part, why these things came upon me. My life-story has already made plain that I have had much prosperity in the work of the Lord. As bright days and seasons as were ever given to a son of Adam were given to me. I could part with the memories and visions of the bright days: it is not so with the gifts of the dark and cloudy

L

days. These latter have let me know by experience that faith can penetrate the darkest clouds. It can prove victorious over every foe.

About this time Weaver received an invitation to carry on Gospel work in a hall in Manchester. The invitation seemed to be of the Lord. It seemed also to offer a permanent sphere of settled usefulness. He removed with his family from Macclesfield to Manchester.

So long as health was given him, all was well. But the terrible strain that he had endured began to tell. The pain in his head became so great that he was unable to preach. There were grave fears that his reason was beginning to tremble on its throne. His devoted wife got him away to Liverpool, to stay with some friends there. He rallied somewhat, but not sufficiently to warrant his taking up the work, so that had to be given up; and with the giving up of the work he said good-bye to a regular income.

Under the necessity of reducing expenditure, the troubled family gave up their home in Manchester, and went to reside in a little cottage in Alderley Edge. But Weaver's convalescence did not continue. Instead of getting better, every day witnessed a change for the worse. Erysipelas at last laid hold upon him, and he was unconscious for seven days and nights. The doctor visited him three or four times a day to see if he were still alive. All hope that he would recover was given up. The children were taken to his bedside to get their final look at him ere he breathed his last. It was an unconscious lump of clay that they looked upon.

The mother had faith to believe that God had a better leave-taking in store for them than that; so she knelt in prayer, and pleaded with God to let the father's consciousness return ere he set out on his long journey; and the prayer was answered. Weaver fell asleep. When he awoke, consciousness had been restored.

But it was a return to new troubles. Two of the children had been seized with small-pox. They lay in the adjoining room. So ill were they, that it was uncertain whether they were not "marked for falling." Nor was that the only new trial. A solicitor's demand for instant payment of £300 lay awaiting his attention. In connection with the arrangements for the work in Manchester, a burden was allowed to fall on Weaver that he should never have been called upon to carry. These new trials made his return to consciousness a sad return. As he himself says:

"There I lay, helpless and alone, apparently forsaken by even those who once seemed likely to prove the staunchest of friends. I was getting better; but my earthly future in those days of darkness was a somewhat cheerless prospect."

But God was remembering his servant. It was a fit time for one of "those good deeds in a naughty world" that remind us that the angels have not yet left the earth. Mr. William Allman, a Cheshire farmer, came one day to that trouble-shadowed cottage, and asked Mrs. Weaver if she were in need of anything. He gave as his reason for coming that the Lord had laid it upon his heart to come and put the question he had asked. Trembling and astonished, Mrs. Weaver told him of the solicitor's demand for the instant payment of £300. The farmer took the demand, went and paid the money, and returned to his farm all unconscious that he had been an angel of God. (Weaver was enabled to repay this loan.)

And he was not the only angel of God that visited that sorely-troubled cottage home. Weaver himself shall tell us of the visit of another, and of what followed thereon.

Mr. John Street, the friend who at the beginning of my itinerant evangelistic work procured me leave of absence from the coal-pit, was the means under God of lifting me out of a gloomier pit than the other had been. He came to see me, and took me with him to his home at Oldham. One day while I was staying there, a Mr. Stansfield came to tea. He was a partner of the firm of Butterworth and Murgatroyd, of Glebe Mills, Hollinwood. He was quite a stranger to me, and I was thus somewhat astonished when he said:

"Mr. Weaver, will you come and live among us, and do what you can in the way of visiting the people around? and my partners and I will stand by you."

I said, "I think my labours in the Lord's work are drawing to a close. I am not able to do much now."

"Well," he said, "we don't want you to do much. Do what you can, and we'll stand by you in the matter of your earthly necessities."

On thinking over the offer, it seemed to me that it did not matter to myself where I spent the little part of life left me; so I agreed to go and hold meetings in the Workmen's Hall on the Lord's day. After I had held meetings for a few Sundays, they took a house for me, and sent vans for my furniture, and settled me in Hollinwood. The place had at that time the reputation of being one of the roughest and wickedest in Lancashire; but even there the Lord had reserved unto Himself a few who had not bowed the knee to Baal. These were anxious for the salvation of their neighbours. They brought me eighty Bibles for free distribution. Mr. Stansfield induced the workpeople to open their houses to us for cottage meetings. I took the Bibles round, distributing them as far as they would go, and I read the Word, and talked to the people as opportunity offered.

One night our cottage meeting was in Bower Lane. The house was so small that I borrowed a chair and went outside and began to sing. People gathered round inquiring who I was, where I came from, and what I was going to do. On the last point they were not left long in the dark. Interest in the mission was awakened. The Lord was with us. Conversions were taking place almost every night. Amongst those who made profession of finding Christ were some of the worst characters in the place. Mr. Stansfield took his stand with me when I went to mission the streets. There was opposition and persecution. I was nicknamed "Butterworth and Company's bull-dog." It only deepened the interest in the mission. Our numbers so increased from week to week that the Institute became too small. My benefactors built a hall for me at a cost of over £3,000. When Dr. Talmage preached in it he said it was the finest mission hall he had ever seen.

The local newspaper gave an exceedingly full account of the proceedings in connection with

THE LAYING OF THE FOUNDATION STONE

of the afore-mentioned hall. It evidently was regarded as an incident of some note in the district. As it was an event of considerable importance in Weaver's life, I give a somewhat detailed account of the story of the day. I get my information from the newspaper report.

It was on a Saturday. The day was fine. Flags were flying from Glebe Mills. The members of the mission met in the tent in Hardman Street at 2.30, and, headed by the Hollinwood Original Brass Band, walked in procession to the site of the building. That a goodly measure of success had been granted to Weaver may be inferred from the fact, that although he had been as yet only a short time at work there, the processionists numbered two hundred and ninety-six. Having arrived at the place where the hall was being built, Weaver, who conducted the proceedings, gave out the hymn, "Rock of Ages." When that had been sung, he engaged in prayer. Thereafter he proceeded to present Mr. Stansfield with a trowel of silver and a mallet of ivory. On the trowel was the inscription:

God so loved the world, that He gave his only-begotten Son, that whosoever believeth in Him should not perish, but have everlasting life.

On the mallet in an inlaid plate were the words:

Presented by the friends of the Hollinwood Mission, conducted by Mr. Richard Weaver, to Edwin Stansfield, Esq., on the occasion of his laying the foundation stone of a Mission Hall, built by the munificence of Messrs. Butterworth and Murgatroyd, Glebe Mills, Hollinwood, July 27th, 1878.

On one side of the stone, which Mr. Stansfield proceeded to lay, was the inscription:

Unto you therefore which believe, Christ is precious; but unto them which be disobedient, the stone which the builders disallowed is made the head of the corner.

On another side of the stone, which was a corner stone, were the words:

This stone was laid by Edwin Stansfield, Esq., 1878.

In the course of his address, Mr. Stansfield said that their object in building that place and calling it a Mission Hall was not in furtherance of any particular creed or doctrine, but for the salvation of the Bible. The plain and simple truths of the Gospel would be declared in that place; and he hoped, if he was spared to see it opened, and the mission located in it, to see it made use of by God as a place for the gathering in of souls.

After Mr. Butterworth had addressed the gathering, Dr. Cranage, of Wellington, spoke, and in the course of his address said that he very much liked to see mission halls. They had one in their town, and it was mainly by the instrumentality of their friend Mr. Weaver that it was built. Mr. Weaver came to Wellington to hold some services, and whilst there he suggested to them the idea of a Mission Hall. They accordingly set to work, and when they had a small balance in hand, they commenced to build. But when the hall was finished they still wanted £50, and for a time they could not see their way. They all earnestly desired to open the mission hall free of debt. There was a young Quaker staying with him at the time, and this friend never ceased to pray to God to send in the remaining £50. It so happened that on the day before that on which the hall was to be opened, the young man ruptured a blood vessel. He was carried into his (Dr.

Cranage's) house, and he died, exclaiming, "My Jesus hath done all things well." They did not know the full meaning of their friend's words at the time, but when his will was read it was found that in it he had bequeathed £50 to their mission hall. Dr. Cranage added that Mr. Weaver opened their hall for them in 1862.

After a hymn and prayer the company adjourned to the Institute for tea. Thereafter a public meeting, presided over by Mr. Stansfield, was held in the Tent. The chairman was supported on the platform by Richard Weaver, Mr. Thos. Wood, and Mr. John Street, of Oldham; Mr. Alfred Butterworth, Springbank, Werneth; and Mr. Roberts, of Liverpool. In the course of his address the chairman alluded to the fact that when Weaver came among them, they, as a body of mission workers, were subjected to much criticism, to cold looks, and to many unkind taunts. It hurt him much, but it also set him scheming how to make the work more effective. When he thought the time had fairly come, he spoke to his partners in the private office about the advisability of building a hall better suited for the work. They were at one with him on that point. Then arose the question, Should the mission people be allowed to carry the burden of building the hall, or should that burden be carried for them? His partners said to him (Mr. Stansfield), "What do you think about it?" He said that the place should be built for the people. There and then they decided to build it. Plans were advertised for. So quietly had the thing been done, that even Mr. Weaver was taken by surprise. When he was shown the plans he thought they were plans for some other building instead of their own. Mr. Stansfield was glad they were fast tiring down the prejudices of their neighbours.

Weaver was the next speaker. He told the story of the way by which he had been led to Hollinwood. In the course of his address he said that when it was suggested that he should come to reside at Hollinwood, his dear wife at first objected. She did not like to leave those beautiful flowers and the splendid landscape scenery which down in Cheshire abounded on every hand. After a little persuasion that difficulty was overcome. With regard to the work he had to confess that it was hard at the start, but with God's help he had been able to wade through it all. He was thankful to say that now he had a good band of devoted workers, and the people were beginning to look at him and to give him a kind word and a shake of the hand when they met him.

Mr. John Street then addressed the assembly. Adverting to Weaver's illness of two years before, he said he received a letter from Mrs. Weaver asking him to go and see her husband. He went and found him in a very weak state indeed. He said to Mr. Weaver in his own old-fashioned way: "Neaw, my lad, it ul noan do fort' ha thi here like this." He accordingly brought him to Oldham, where he had got fairly strong and had laid the foundation of a great work.

Mr. Alfred Butterworth said nobody felt prouder than he at being present on that occasion. He recollected the time before he gave himself to God, that his whole aim and ambition was to get money, and his principal study seemed to be how to adopt plans by which he might more readily fill his coffers. But he was glad to say a very important change had been wrought in him. He now looked upon wealth as a thing of secondary importance; as the love of it was likely at times to turn their thoughts from those great and high and noble considerations which ought to be every Christian's deepest concern. It required a person to be always on his guard lest he should find himself going in the wrong path.

Other speeches in like spirit followed, and the proceedings closed in the usual manner.

The following are the testimonies of two of the Hollinwood converts:

From Jammie Taylor.

Formerly there was at the top of Hollinwood what they called the "Road End Gang," and there were certain gentlemen who used to come every Sunday afternoon and hold cottage meetings. One Sunday afternoon one of them came amongst this gang, giving tracts, and inviting us to the cottage meeting with him. When we got to the door and saw that the place was full of women and other people, we turned back again. Then we went back to the top of the street, and we commenced to gamble again in the way of tossing, and I won eighteenpence with it. After the meeting was over, we stood at the end of the street, and this gentleman came to us and said to me, "Don't you think you would have been better if you had been in the meeting with us this afternoon?" I said "No." And he said, "For why?" and I said, "For this reason, while you have been in the meeting I have won eighteenpence with tossing." He said, "You have sold your soul for eighteenpence!" and I said that if I had, I would sell it again for eighteenpence if I had the chance.

Then he said there was a man preaching at the Hollinwood Institute, named Richard Weaver, and he invited us to go and listen to him; and we went, and when we got there a lot of us sat in a corner where there was a fireplace. There was a man with a silk hat and we commenced to get cinders to spin at this silk hat.

Mr. Weaver spied us out from the platform, and he knew me by coming and visiting my father when he was sick, and he exposed me to that extent that when I left the meeting I commenced to swear, and I threatened that if I had him I'd shove him in the canal. The week following, I don't know how it was, but I was led to the same place again; and that night, instead of throwing the preacher into the canal, the Lord came with his great, mighty power through the preacher, and I fell into the fountain. That is now over nineteen years since, and I have never regretted one moment of serving God.

From John Isherwood.

For many years I was a member of the Hollinwood Working Men's Institute. I used to play at billiards, bowling, and card-playing. One night I was playing at billiards, and the billiard-room was propped up with four props. While playing, one of these props was in the way of the cue. I made inquiries from Mr. Hardman, the man in charge of the Club, what was the matter that the props were up again, and he told me that the converted collier, Mr. Weaver, was coming to preach in the room above. After the game was over, I went upstairs out of curiosity, as I was a collier myself, and had heard so much of Richard Weaver. After the singing and praying was over, he commenced to preach about Martha and Mary; and the earnestness of the man was so great that I came to the conclusion that he had gone out of his mind. After speaking at home about him and about his earnestness, I went again; and for six months, Sunday after Sunday, I kept going. I was still blind to my sins. At last a time came when Weaver as an instrument in God's hands preached from the old text, "Thou art weighed in the balance and found wanting." I was invited to stay to the prayer meeting; I went instead to the "Filho," and called for a glass of bitter beer; but the Spirit of God was now working upon me through the words of the preacher in such force that I went home, and if they haven't removed the beer that I called for nineteen years ago, it is there still! Little did I think at the time when I put the cue into the rack and went to hear him that I should work with him. I am in the work yet, and still labouring in the same hall. For seven years I have been superintendent of the Hollinwood Mission Hall.

Introduction to Dr. Talmage, of America.

The following remarks were made by Dr. Talmage on his return to America after one of his visits to this country. The account is reprinted from *The Signal*:—

I had great desire to see the much talked about, often condemned, but divinely honoured Richard Weaver, the English Evangelist. He has for many years been stirring the hearts of vast multitudes. It has been no unusual thing for him to address ten thousand people in the open-air, and to have hundreds under one sermon converted. "Is it not strange," I often said, "that I see nothing of Richard Weaver." He had for years paused in his itinerant work, and been preaching in a large hall in Hollinwood, near Oldham.

At last I found him coming out of the stables of one of my hosts (Dr. Cranage, of Wellington, Salop), where he had been looking at the horses. I heard him singing before I saw him. We greeted each other like old friends. "You must go to Hollinwood," he said. "I cannot go," was the reply. "I have but one day, and that next Saturday, to rest in before I leave England, and I must rest or die."

By this time we had reached the house. He got down on his knees, and said: "O Lord, show this man that it is his duty to go to Hollinwood." Rising, he said: "This is my excuse for demanding that you go. It will be the neediest audience that you have seen in England. All poor, and the Lord's poor, and you have not seen England till you have seen my humble Mission Hall." After further consideration I accepted the invitation to preach on the Saturday afternoon. Arrived at Hollinwood, we had a delightful time. Richard Weaver is one of the most magnetic men I ever met. He recited reminiscences, and sang for me, and did everything except tell the story of the Lost Sheep. I said to him: "I have heard and read much about the way you tell that story"; but he declined, saying that he needed the inspiration of a large audience before him to do it well. True to his statement, the people in the hall were the Lord's poor. I never enjoyed preaching more than that afternoon to that unpretending audience. A gentleman (one of the partners who built the hall) played the organ. As I was leaving for the train, he handed me an envelope. I said, "Excuse me, I cannot take that. I suppose it is to meet my expenses. I came down here to serve Richard Weaver, and I will pay my own expenses." He replied, "You do not know what the letter contains. Put it in your pocket." Arriving at the station, I opened the letter, and was surprised more than I can tell, for it contained one hundred pounds.

When Dr. Talmage preached in the Hall, he commenced his address by saying that when quite a young man, his mother one day gave him a little book entitled, "The Life of Richard Weaver." She said, "De Witt, read this; and if ever you go to England, be sure and meet with this man whom God has so blessed." "And," Dr. Talmage continued, "here we are, Richard Weaver and myself, on the same platform, serving the same God, preaching the same Gospel, and bound for the same Heaven." His text was "Come thou and all thy house into the ark." According to our informant, he preached a sermon of such power and pathos that it can never be forgotten by those who had the privilege of hearing it.

During Weaver's sojourn at Hollinwood, when visiting on one occasion at the house of his dear old friend, Dr. Cranage, he met a converted Parsee, Mr. M. H. Mody, of Bombay. He was of the highest birth, and ranked as an Indian prince; but because of his conversion to Christianity, he had been cut off and persecuted by his friends and relatives. Weaver introduced him to those who had built the Hall for, and had proved such friends to, himself. Through their munificence Mr. Mody was sent out to Bombay to labour for Christ among his own people, the Parsees, and his work has been blessed of God to many souls.

It should also be said that the Bible used by Richard

up till the day of his death, was presented to him when he entered upon his labours at Hollinwood. The bond of love that existed between him and his mission people was wonderful, and accounts for the greatness of the work that was through him accomplished there. Many of his friends say that of all the works which God did through Richard Weaver, the work at Hollinwood is one of the mightiest in its results.

Mr. Weaver's narrative proceeds:

Now I thought, and they thought, that I was settled there for life; but God had ordered it otherwise. Friends from London and other parts of England, and from Ireland, Scotland, and Wales, kept pleading with me to give up the Hollinwood mission, and go up and down the country as before. At last the appeals became so pressing that I was driven to the conclusion that the Lord was calling me. After prayer and conversation with my brother Stansfield, I decided to go.

It cost me a great struggle to leave the place where I had lived and laboured for five happy years, and the people that I loved as my children in the Gospel. Many times since, and especially since my health failed me, have I found myself wishing I had remained. They were so kind to me. They saw to all my earthly wants, so that I was free to devote my time and strength to the work. There was nothing that they could do for me that they did not do; no kindness that man could wish that they did not show. I have often wished myself back among them; but in deciding as I did, I followed such light as I had, and have not the slightest doubt that I was led in the right path. I believe that all is well.

XI.
A True Comrade.

THE first place Weaver visited on leaving Hollinwood was Dr. Barnardo's "Edinburgh Castle," in the East of London. The following is taken from a report of an address which he delivered there on the evening of the Derby Day, 1881:—

I went to-day into a hairdresser's shop in Newgate Street. The first thing the barber said was:

"Are you going to the Derby?"

I looked at him, setting my eyes firmly upon him, and said, "Blessed is the man that walketh not in the counsel of the ungodly, nor standeth in the way of sinners, nor sitteth in the seat of the scornful, but his delight is in the law of the Lord."

The barber shaved me in silence.

How the people were flocking past as I came along, evidently rushing to the Races! Now, my dear friends, what they call "pleasure" is only sadness, and grief, and anxiety. I, for one, don't believe in gambling at all. I believe it to be downright dishonesty and theft.

A GAMBLER IS ONLY A RESPECTABLE THIEF;

and he ought to go and live in St. Giles', along with other thieves. No gambler gambles for the benefit of other people. It is only for himself; and he doesn't care whose money he gets so that he gets it. It doesn't matter to him who goes to the wall if only he himself is all right. They may make fun of Sir Wilfrid Lawson, with his opposition to the adjournment of Parliament on such an occasion; but he is right. It is a disgrace to our country that its government should be in the hands of men who adjourn Parliament for "the Derby." If we are a Christian community, we should act worthy of the name we bear.

While I was preaching at Dr. Barnardo's I stayed with a friend whose house had been my home during all my sojourns in the great city. He sent an invitation to my wife to join me. She came, bringing our three youngest children with her. A month after coming up to London she became unwell, and returned home with the children. I was under promise to conduct a mission in Mr. Charrington's Assembly Hall, Mile End Road, and remained in London for that purpose.

One day, while at prayer, I felt impressed that the Lord was about to take my wife to Himself. I told the people I believed I had a great trial before me. When I had done speaking, a lady said to me, "You should try to dispel such thoughts as these." Still the presentiment remained. I went home. When I entered the house I said to my niece:

"Where's your aunt?"

"In bed, uncle," was the answer.

Without taking off hat or coat, I walked upstairs, and was received with a smile and a kiss. I said:

"Sarah, how are you?"

She replied that she thought she was better. In another room lay our youngest child, ill of scarlatina. That was on the Monday. On the Thursday I sent for other doctors, that a consultation might be held. When they came downstairs, they said:

"Mr. Weaver, you must prepare for the worst."

Next day my wife lay there: our eldest son Sam sat beside her, holding her right hand, and looking at his mother. The doctor sat in a chair near. Speaking to our son, he said he could do no more. The youth said to his mother:

"Mother, Dr. Sparrow has done all he can."

She said, "Have you, Doctor?"

He replied, "Yes, Mrs. Weaver."

She said, "God bless you, Doctor; I shall soon be in heaven with my Saviour. Will you meet me there?"

"I hope so, Mrs. Weaver," was the reply.

She tenderly urged him to have his *hope* exchanged for assurance. She pleaded that He who shed his precious blood was worthy of *trust*.

The doctor went away, and she sent for some of our neighbours. Among those who came were my benefactor, Mr. Stansfield, and his good wife. She said to him:

"Mr. Stansfield, you have been very kind to me and mine; and I pray God to reward you here and hereafter. You will meet me in heaven, won't you, Mr. Stansfield?"

He said, "Yes, Mrs. Weaver."

A friend who had been a great drunkard, but had been brought to Christ, came with his wife. When they entered the room, my wife said to him:

"I shall soon be in heaven; will you meet me there?"

He said, "Yes, Mrs. Weaver."

She turned to his wife, saying, "Kiss me."

She did so, and was then asked the same question. She could not say that her sins were forgiven; so her answer was, "I hope I shall."

"Hope! The blood of Jesus never fails. Kiss me again!"

It was done. Again she was asked the pointed question: "Will you meet me in heaven?" Many a time was the question repeated, for my wife would not let her go. At last her friend broke down, and cried out:

"The Lord help me, Mrs. Weaver. I *will* meet you in heaven."

Two friends who had been telegraphed for arrived, and were shown into her room. I was dumb. My wife greeted them with the request that she had been making of all the others. One of them turned to me and said, "To be here is to be in the antechamber of heaven."

I saw that her life was ebbing fast. I went to the bedside, on which was lying the wife that had lived with me more than thirty years. She had rejoiced in my joy. She had wept with me in my sorrow. Many times when I had been cast down, she had comforted and cheered me. Often had she risen from her bed in the small hours of the morning to plead with God for me. She was the mother of my six children.

I said, "Sarah, have you given us all up?"

She said, "I wonder at you, Richard. I gave our children to the Lord when they were born; and I shall meet them all in heaven." She went on to say: "There are three things I want you to promise me."

I asked, "What are they?"

"First, you will bury me in Ardwick Cemetery, in the grave of my mother; it will hold two—you and me."

I said, "That shall be done."

"Second, you will be as kind to our niece as to our own children. She has been a good girl to me."

"That shall be done."

"Third, you will try after I am dead and gone to win more souls to Christ than you have done while I was living. *And, if I can, I will pray for you in heaven.*"

I said, "That shall be done."

Many times since, when I have seen the mighty power of God on the congregations I have been addressing, I have believed that my wife was pleading with Jesus for me.

Then turning to her children, she said:

> "What is there here to court my stay
> Or hold me back from home,
> While angels beckon me away,
> And Jesus bids me come?"

Whispering the words, "Precious blood," she departed to be for ever with the Lord.

No man knows the value of a good wife till he has lost her. It was after mine had gone that I made the discovery that I had lost my right arm of power, and wisdom, and counsel.

BENDIGO.

As an example of one of the ways in which my wife was unto me a true helpmeet in the work of the Lord, I will narrate the story of the conversion of a notable character who went by the name of "Bendigo." His real name was William Thompson. He was a great prize-fighter. In my own unconverted days I had often bet on his fights. At his birth he was one of triplets. He was brought up as a heathen, and permitted to run about and do as he liked. He told me he never had a shoe on his foot, nor any clothes worth speaking of, till he was in his teens.

From his youth he had a very strong propensity for fighting. He fought twenty-seven prize-fights, and he won them all. He stood some five feet ten inches high; but what weight he was I cannot say. He could throw a stone two hundred yards. He could heave half a brick across the river Trent, at Nottingham, where it is seventy yards in width. There was hardly a field in the neighbourhood of Nottingham that he could not throw a cricket ball over. Though he could not read a word, he was in the earlier of his fighting years noted for his temperate habits and truthful disposition. He thought that God had given him the ability to fight, that he might win money to keep his mother out of the workhouse. No one ever taught him the art of boxing; nor did he imitate any man's style.

Before he went into a fight he used to go down on his knees and ask the Lord to allow him to win, for his mother's sake. But he fell from the paths of temperance. He had saved a little money, and had placed it in the hands of one who professed great friendship for him. But the profession was hollow. He robbed Bendigo of it all save £30, and the too-trustful fighter was so cast down at the shameful way in which he had been treated, that in a fit of recklessness he took his £30 and began a drinking spree, which ended in his being brought before the magistrates.

After this he became careless. The white flower of his reputation had become so soiled that he despaired of its restoration. He was continually in trouble, and often in prison. It had been thus with him for a long time, when I went to Nottingham to preach. I wanted to see Bendigo; but when I told a brother in Christ about my desire he simply laughed at me and said:

"It's no use. He'll simply tell you that the Lord gave him the power to fight to keep his mother out of the workhouse."

I failed to obtain an interview. Ten years later, on the invitation of kind friends, I returned to conduct a mission in the town in the neighbourhood of which was Bendigo's home. On Thursday afternoon I was praying about the meeting that I was to conduct in the evening. To my astonishment, I could not think of any text from which to speak to the crowd that would gather in the hall where I was to preach. My mind was full of Bendigo. The only voice that seemed to me to come from heaven was a voice which said:

"Pray for old Bendigo."

Presently I was called to my tea. At the table I asked my host if he could tell me where old Bendigo was.

"In prison," he said. "At least, if he is not there he has only just come out, and they are after him with a warrant to put him in again."

I said, "I believe God is going to save him. I can think about nothing, pray about no one, save this old man. Will you go with me to-morrow to see the Mayor and get me permission to visit Bendigo in his cell?"

My host said, "Yes, I will go; but I know it's of no use to attempt the conversion of Bendigo," and he laughed. The want of faith vexed me, but I only said,

"Sir, I believe God is about to save Bendigo."

It was the month of February. There had been a heavy fall of snow; so when the hour of meeting drew on, I was driven to the hall. The young man who opened the cab-door, said:

"Who do you think is at the meeting to-night?"

I said, "I don't know."

He said, "Old Bendigo."

On making inquiries, I found that he had come out of prison only that morning. Some of his old chums and companions, who went by the name of "Nottingham lambs," had gone to the prison gates to welcome him out. In addition to these, a man of some wealth, who had heard me preach, and thought my preaching would help Bendigo, had also gone to the prison gates at the hour when prisoners are discharged. When Bendigo made his appearance, his old "pals" went forward and shook hands with him, and said:

"Come along, Bill; we've got a breakfast ready for thee—warm ale and beef-steaks. Come!"

Mr. W—— also stepped forward and said, "No, don't go, Thompson; I want you to come with me. I have got a capital breakfast prepared for you; and I want you to go to-night and hear a man preach in the Temperance Hall. He was formerly a collier and a prize-fighter. They used to call him 'Undaunted Dick.'"

Bendigo said, "Mr. W——, I'll go with thee;" and thus Bendigo was led to the meeting.

I went in, got on the platform, and looked round for Bendigo. Though I had never seen him before, I had no difficulty in picking him out. I called to him to come and take a seat on the platform by my side. He walked limping on to the platform. His limp was due to his having broken one of his knee-caps when he was turning a somersault before one of his fights. He sat by my side as I preached. My watch lay on the table. He kept lifting it, and looking at it. A gentleman whispered:

"Mind your watch, or Bendigo will have it."

I whispered back, "Never mind; God will give me another."

By-and-by Bendigo became restless and said he must leave, or the train would be going without him. He lived at a place named Beeston, about four miles out of Nottingham. I told him to sit still, and if he missed his train I would send him home in a cab. Next morning he had to appear before the magistrate. The usual penalty—six weeks or two guineas—was imposed. Mr. W—— paid his fine, and he was back in the hall in the evening. He wept as I spoke. Next day I went to see him in his cottage home. It was like a little museum, so filled was it with presents of one kind and another. I spent the afternoon pleading with God for him, and pleading with him for God. When I left he seemed thoughtful. Next day was Sabbath, and the last of the days of my mission. At the evening service the place was crowded long before the hour. A large number stood round the door unable to gain admittance. Seeing the prize-fighter approach they cried:

"Here comes old Bendigo: make way for him!"

He was planted once more on the platform by my side. My theme was—God's love to even the chief of sinners. God's Spirit was at work. When I had done speaking, Bendigo dropped on his knees before that vast concourse of people, and cried to God for mercy. His prayer was:

"O Lord, if Thou couldst save a man like 'Undaunted Dick,' Thou canst save me."

The people shouted, "God bless old Bill!"

Some of them were weeping; some were laughing—in each case I believe it was for joy. Bendigo got up from his knees, and said:

"What are you laughing at? I have fought for you, haven't I?"

"Yes, Bill."

"Well, I will pray for you now."

It came into my mind to take Bendigo home to Cheshire with me. I said:

"Friends, it has come into my mind to take Bendigo home with me, if he will go."

They cried, "God bless you, Mr. Weaver."

Bendigo said, "I will go, Daddy." He called me "Daddy," though I was his junior by some years.

Morning came. I went out with my host to say good-bye to a few friends before I started for Cheshire. When we returned Bendigo had arrived. My hostess called me into another room, and said:

"Mr. Weaver, if I were in your place I would not take Bendigo home. He's a walking nuisance."

By-and-by came a message from Bendigo's brother telling me not to take his brother Bill to my home, as he would only insult us all. I thought if I could get him away from his old companions and friends, there would be more of a chance for him, so I stuck to my resolution. I got him to take a bath. We had him rigged out in a new suit—underclothes and overclothes, for both were needed. In company with a friend named Mr. Dupe, we set forth for Cheshire. When we were passing Alton Towers, Bendigo said:

"I am so hungry, Daddy."

I said, "Cheer up; we'll have some shrimp pie when we get home."

Turning to Mr. Dupe, he said:

"I shall want something better than shrimp pie when we get there."

We reached home. Pointing to some sides of bacon that hung overhead, and speaking to Mr. Dupe, he said:

"Jim, shrimp pie! shrimp pie!"

Some time afterwards, when we were alone, my wife said to me:

"Richard, you have brought many a rough character here, but this one seems to be the masterpiece. I shall be afraid to stay in the same house with him."

I said, "The Lord has turned the lion into a lamb."

But Bendigo had not as yet entered into light. That evening passed away. We had prayers, and retired to rest. Next evening came. Mr. Dupe, my wife, and I, were in the study. Bendigo was in the dining-room with the children. Thinking we would like to see how they were getting on, we slipped noiselessly to the door of the dining room. With the wisdom of those who lock the door of the stable after the steed is stolen, we had put a guard around the fireplace after our little Frankie had burnt his right hand through falling into the fire.

It was very cold. The children were on their knees around the fire-guard. They were saying their child prayers before they retired to rest. Bendigo was kneeling with them. Reginald, as the eldest of the young children, was leading the others.

We heard him say, "Lord, bless father."

To our astonishment, Bendigo also said, "Lord, bless father."

"Lord, bless mother," said the boy.

"Lord, bless mother," said Bendigo.

The boy prayed for his friends one by one, and the petitions were repeated by Bendigo. Then came "Lord, bless Bendigo."

"Lord, bless Bendigo," said poor Bendigo.

"They say Bendigo is a bad man, Lord," said the boy.

"They say Bendigo is a bad man, Lord, and it's true," said the man.

"But Thou canst save Bendigo," said the boy.

"But Thou canst save Bendigo," repeated the man.

"Thy blood was shed for Bendigo," said the boy.

"Thy blood was shed for Bendigo," said the man.

"Lord, save Bendigo to-night," said the boy, concluding his little prayer.

"Lord, save Bendigo to-night," said the man, in tones of unmistakable earnestness.

Mr. Dupe said, "Praise the Lord!" My wife wept. My heart was bowed in worship at the manifestation of Jesus' power to save that mine own eyes were beholding. They arose from their knees. Bendigo took our youngest son into his arms, and carried him round the room, sighing:

"Oh that I had been taught in my childhood to pray, and to love God. How different my life would have been!"

My wife made her appearance. Bendigo turned to her, and said:

"God bless you, madam! Oh that I had been brought

up as these children are being brought up! What a life I have lived! But I am in heaven now. I am in heaven now."

And the penitent prize-fighter knelt once more, and laid his head on the fire-guard, and sobbed like a little child. The heart of a little child was given unto him. He arose from his knees born of God.

Changed thus by Divine grace, he had now no greater delight than to hear the Word of God. He kept our Reginald so closely engaged reading it to him that the boy's sight failed him for a time. Bendigo travelled with me, and sat by my side on platforms in Liverpool, London, Birmingham, Manchester, Rochdale, Hanley, Derby, Leicester, and in many other places. Some that no words of mine could reach were unable to resist the testimony of old Bendigo. To see him " clothed and in his right mind" was to them nothing short of a miracle of saving grace. Conviction laid hold of them, and they fled for refuge to Bendigo's Saviour.

Returning home, he joined the Good Templars, and obtained complete mastery over the drink that once had held him in chains. His desire for it was completely taken away.

At last, one day whilst coming down from the attic of the little cot at Beeston, where he lived, he slipped at the turn of the stairs and fell to the bottom. Several ribs were broken, and one of the broken ribs had pierced his lungs. The news spread that Bendigo was dying. Rich and poor, Christians and worldlings—for he was esteemed by all—went to see him. Amongst those who visited him was the ex-pugilist, Harry Pawson, who had fought Tom Sayers. The dying man put out his hand to welcome his old friend, and said:

"Harry, will you meet me in heaven?"

"I am too bad, Bill."

"You have never been so bad as me, Harry; and if the Lord could pardon me, He can pardon you. Harry, promise to meet me in heaven."

"I am too bad," said Harry again.

But Bendigo would not give him up. Looking appealingly to him he said:

"Harry, give me a kiss as a promise that you will meet me in heaven."

The story as I have given it is from the lips of a gentleman who was present at the interview. My informant told me that when Harry Pawson bent, with weeping eyes, over old Bendigo on his dying bed and kissed him, his own eyes filled. To see these old warriors bidding each other such a farewell was more than he could bear.

After Harry had given the kiss that was to Bendigo a promise that his friend would meet him in heaven, the dying prize-fighter did his best to sing these two lines:

> For you must be a lover of the Lord,
> Or you won't go to heaven when you die.

They were almost his last words. Soon after singing them, he departed to be with Christ.

The aldermen of Nottingham, at their own expense, gave his remains an imposing public funeral. He was buried, according to his own wish, in his mother's grave. Over the grave they erected a massive tombstone, on which is sculptured—

A LION AT REST.

XII.

Revisiting former Battle-fields.

AFTER a campaign of many months in London, we find Weaver in the North of England. In the pages of *The Christian* we see accounts of successful Missions that he conducted in Newcastle, Blyth, Scotswood, Spennymoor, Shildon, Crook, etc.

On the invitation of Mr. Quarrier, of The Orphan Homes of Scotland, he crossed the Border to conduct a five weeks' mission in the second city of the kingdom. After receiving Weaver's promise to come to Glasgow, the Orphans' friend and a few of his workers set about securing halls for the Sabbath services. They were looking at St. Andrew's Hall—the largest in the city—and discussing its suitability for the eleven o'clock meeting. One of the workers said:

"We need not take this: we could not fill it."

In his own characteristic way, Mr. Quarrier replied:

"We will take the hall, and leave the Lord to fill it."

So the hall was taken, and Mr. Quarrier's faith had its justifying reward. When the hour of meeting came the place was filled in every corner. A meeting of workers gathered in the hall of The Orphan Home, to welcome Richard on the evening of his arrival in Glasgow. The building was crowded, not only with inhabitants of Glasgow but also with some who had come several miles to see their old friend, and in many cases their spiritual father. When the evangelist made his appearance, the whole congregation rose to their feet and sang,

      Praise God, from whom all blessings flow.

After overcoming the emotion produced by so cordial a welcome, Weaver's eye caught the following motto on the wall: "If ye shall ask anything in My name, I will do it." Catching up the words "I will do it," he dwelt on the fact that if souls were to be converted in Glasgow—and of that he had not the slightest doubt—it must be the Lord's doing. That was a work that was beyond man's power.

The following account of the mission is taken from the pages of Mr. Quarrier's narrative for that year (1881-2):—

On the 19th of November, Richard Weaver began five weeks' special services with us. For many years we had been observing how the Lord was using this servant of his to the working people in many parts of England, and having satisfied ourselves as to his standing, and believing that God would bless him here also to the same class, we invited him to come. The thousands that flocked to hear him filled the three largest halls—the St. Andrew's, the City, and the National—in our city. Every Sabbath witnessed to the fact that he had not lost his old power to get and hold large audiences. Trial had sanctified the vessel, and made him more fitted to tell out the old, old story. We have had large experience of evangelists, and believe there are few so well qualified to speak to the working classes as Richard Weaver. During the five weeks he was with us he conducted over fifty meetings, and at every one of them there were anxious inquirers at the close; and not a few who had passed from death unto life while the meeting was going on. It was pleasing to see the hundreds, as the result of his former work in this city, who came to welcome him. Standing fruit is the best testimony of usefulness in the Master's service that any one can have.

Many were loud in their thanks to us for bringing him to the city. If we had done it for the praise of men, we might have been lifted up; but our only object was to make Christ known to the perishing by using those whom God honours. From the beginning we have sought to work with all who love the Lord Jesus, and we welcome all whom God uses in the winning of souls.

In a conversation that I had with Mr. Quarrier about his invitation of Weaver, I was not astonished at the discovery that the Orphans' friend had not acted without consulting his Urim and Thummim. For a long time he had had it laid on his heart to invite Weaver. The vision was so persistent that it seemed to him to be "of the Lord." But he did not act without spreading out his Gideon's fleece. He asked the Lord, if it really were his desire that Weaver should be invited, to send means for the necessary expenses in such abundance that there could be no mistake. The money came in. Thereupon Mr. Quarrier felt that he need not confer with flesh and blood. He had received his orders, and he obeyed.

While health was given him, a visit to Glasgow under Mr. Quarrier's auspices was an annual occurrence. Once Mr. Quarrier had taken the lead, and the step had received such an abundant justification as those first five weeks gave it, other invitations came pouring in on the evangelist. Amongst these was an invitation from a few old friends in Edinburgh. Mr. Napier was the bearer of the invitation. He gives the following report of the financial arrangement:—

"I asked him of his charges." In reply, he said, "Is Christ dead?" I, of course, said, "No." Then said he, "He will look after all that. If we do our duty, the Lord will do his."

The Drill Hall was engaged for the Sunday evening. It is supposed to hold about six thousand. It was packed to the door.

Weaver's poet laureate was still to the fore; and at the meeting held to bid him good-bye, the following verses were read:—

> We hail thee with gladness, dear Weaver, again
>   To Edina the scene of thy labours of yore;
> Thy presence amongst us will gladly constrain
>   The chords of my harp to re-vibrate once more.
>
> We welcome thee back to old Scotland again,
>   To the land of the covenants, sacred and dear,
> Where martyrs have bled the pure cause to maintain,
>   And truth shone out bright as the firmament clear.
>
> In greeting thee, Richard, we think of the past,
>   When the thousands were moved by thy eloquence great;
> When thy words reached the hearts of the multitudes vast,
>   And made the ungodly with terror to quake.
>
> Though now we behold thee with age on thy head,
>   No longer retaining the freshness of youth,
> Yet a Power is upon thee that rouses the dead,
>   And brings the poor wanderers back to the Truth.
>
> In gladness we lift up our hearts unto God,
>   And prayerfully gather around you to-night,
> To meet you and cheer you and send you abroad
>   More souls to reclaim to the kingdom of light.

By the time of the farewell meeting held in the following year, the heart of the poet was somewhat sore because of the continued absence of many that he expected to see by Weaver's side. To these he makes a passing reference, and then concludes as follows:—

> Whoe'er can forget the bright days of the past,
>   When his words held together the multitude vast!
> In our fields and our halls they gathered to hear
>   And shed o'er the Gospel's sweet story a tear.

> Farewell, then, once more; thy old friends are now few:
> May those that surround thee be gallant and true!
> May Heaven still bless thee, and lengthen thy day,
> To deliver poor sinners from Satan's vile sway!

In connection with those later Edinburgh campaigns, it may be mentioned that the late Dr. Moxey threw himself heartily into the work. In addition, he advised his elocution pupils if they wanted an example of natural oratory, to go and hear Richard Weaver.

On the invitation of the Ayrshire Christian Union he held meetings in Ayr, Maybole, and Kilmarnock. Still following the traces of him that abound in the pages of *The Christian*, we find him next in the North of England, conducting missions in Jarrow, Durham, Willington, and Barrow-in-Furness. Thereafter he visits Wales, and conducts missions in Swansea, in Tonypandy, Cardiff, and Pontypridd. Then we find him in London, conducting special services in various parts of the great metropolis; after this at Belfast, where a blessed work is begun. A few weeks later we see him in the thick of the fight in Liverpool. Blessing attends him wherever he goes. Stirring and interesting incidents occur in great abundance; but as the reader is probably of opinion that he has already had enough of these, I content myself with a pen portrait of the evangelist as he appeared at this period of his life to an able limner, the Rev. Hopper Joplin. It is an eloquent example of the greatness of the impression made by Weaver on his co-workers.

In reproducing the pen portrait I have been compelled from want of space to condense it. In the process the sketch has doubtless suffered considerably.

Those who wish to see it in full as it appears in the original will find it in the files of *The Jarrow Guardian*. The following is the substance of Mr. Joplin's sketch:—

"It was to be expected that time would have wrought some changes upon the popular evangelist. So it has. When he came upon the platform of the Mechanics' Hall on Sunday afternoon it was soon apparent that he is not the man he was twenty years ago. His hair is now white and he complains of a trouble at the heart. This said, I cannot say that I see much difference in his preaching. He seems to have the same power, and his voice does not appear to have lost any of its compass.

"He seems to have been born for his work. He is well built, has a strong constitution, and possesses a remarkably powerful voice. His voice is well managed; he uses it to the best advantage. When appealing to his audience it rolls along in trumpet tones. He is a true orator. He has complete control over his congregation, and keeps them in his powerful grip. He makes them laugh and cry at will. He sways them as the wind sways the standing corn. This is not done mechanically, it is heart speaking to heart. He *talks* to the people. He does not attempt sermonizing, nor does he give essays and learned disquisitions; but he is a true preacher.

"Perhaps his great *forte* is in telling stories. He announces his text, and after having made plain its connections, he seeks to illustrate it. His illustrations are peculiar to himself. They are composed of incidents which have come under his own notice. He does not deal with second-hand anecdotes. It is therefore refreshing to hear from a man's lips, incidents which have come under his own observation. I never heard any one who could relate a story with such effect. I am sure tears, during the last few days, have moistened many eyes that have not known what it was to weep for many a year. It is well for a man to have the better part of his nature stirred up now and again, and I know no man who can do it better than 'the converted collier.'

"Like a master musician, he can bring out the sweetest notes. Many people wonder, and ask, 'What is the secret of Weaver's success?' I think it is due to his marvellous sympathy. He is not a learned man. He does not preach sermons after the fashion of ministers. A working-man himself, he addresses his audience as such, and does it in phrases with which they are familiar; and he begets their sympathy by his downright homeliness. His rendering of Bible stories is very effective; he reduces them to every-day occurrences. He told the story of the Lost Sheep the other night as few men could tell it.

"He is *one of the fathers of the evangelistic movement of the present day*; and I doubt not when the history of the Revival Movement of the latter part of this century is written, Richard Weaver will have assigned to him his true place."

In the same article Mr. Joplin gives us also a portrait of a Weaver crowd from the point of view of one of the crowd. It is such a vivid description of the bigness of the wave that accompanied Weaver's course through the sea of humanity, that I insert it almost in full. It is given by Mr. Joplin as his recollections of the first time he heard Weaver some twenty years before. He was only a tiny school lad at the time.

"I got permission to take a holiday to go and hear the man who was creating such a stir throughout the country. I set off alone, took the train, got to Newcastle, followed the crowd, and soon found myself one of some hundreds who were anxiously awaiting the opening of the doors of the large Town Hall. All sorts of people were there. They had come from the office, the shop, the factory, and the mine, to hear 'the converted collier' preach. It was more like a holiday than an ordinary working day. The crowd was at its best; everybody seemed happy. Now there was a laugh at some enthusiastic brother from the country; then there was a snatch of some popular Revival melody; then the usual sally, as though they would force the doors.

"At length the great moment arrived—the moment when you unconsciously draw yourself up, button your clothes tight about you, adjust your coat-tails, and get ready for the struggle. The doors were thrown open, and everybody wanted to get in first. There was the usual scramble, and the familiar cries, men howling and women screaming; but it is everybody for himself. It was my first experience of the power and selfishness of a crowd. I gave myself up to it. What else could I do? It is of little use fighting the crowd; go with it, and it will land you somewhere. It landed me just where I wanted to be—right in the middle of the hall. But it had been a 'crushing' experience. I felt more dead than alive.

"I remember, when I found myself in a comfortable seat, putting my hand to my side to feel if all my ribs were gone. I felt a strange sensation down about that part. But they seemed to be all there still, and not one of them broken. It did seem, however, that my vest had suddenly become too large for me. I wore knickerbockers, and they were fastened, not with the orthodox braces, but were instead buttoned on to my vest. Oh, that crowd! it had robbed me of some of those buttons, and I was doomed to feel for the remainder of that day a great want and a great danger. I was certain of one thing—that the 'great crowd' had taken what little there was of me and squeezed it into the smallest possible compass. I cannot say that I have fully recovered from that crushing yet.

"In spite of it all, however, I was soon enjoying the hymns which were started impromptu by the congregation and sung with the greatest enthusiasm. It is a happy way of spending an hour. You must fill up the time in some way or other. It seems to be a question of putting your fingers in your mouth or singing. I prefer singing."

In the earlier months of 1884 Weaver began to be troubled about his duty to his motherless children. He felt that he ought to be to them at once a father and a mother; but he was called away from home so much that he was bereft of the opportunity usually given to the earthly father. He had a home for them, and one of the best of housekeepers; but to him a home without a mother was like a house without a roof. He thought if he could find some godly woman willing to unite her interests with his, his children would be even better cared for. He did find such a woman in Miss Needham, of Leek, and was married to her on April 3rd, 1884. The sentence from her letter that I have given in the Preface is ample evidence of her sympathy with Richard in his life work. We do not wonder that he was happy in this marriage also. As the years passed on, he had increasing reason, with Addison, to give God thanks for "The kind and faithful friend that doubled all his store." And well was it for him and his that he had such an helpmeet. In his later years he was a sorely-tried man. He had no lack of invitations to conduct missions, but he had a sad lack of physical health. In the earlier years of his work for God, he had made terrible drafts on his nervous system. The bill had now to be paid: and in much pain and weakness, and many breaks of engagements, it was paid. Latterly he counted himself happy if he could work for twelve or thirteen weeks out of the fifty-two. Yet the gleanings of his life were richer than the full vintage of many an Abiezer. He still was made use of to turn many unto righteousness.

These decisions for Christ gladdened his heart and filled his mouth with praise; but they did not feed and clothe and house himself and his family. The Lord allowed him to suffer from continuous broken health during the later years of his life; and broken health, long continued, ultimately came to mean financial strain; and the latter, to one like Weaver, who wished to owe no man anything but love, was a pain more difficult to bear than the physical. He became weary. He began to rejoice in the fact that he was only a stranger and a pilgrim in the earth. He had his "*lodgings* in Cheshire," but his "*home* was in heaven."

XIII.

Stones from Weaver's Sling.

FOR the sake of those readers who never had the privilege of hearing Weaver, I add a few extracts from his addresses. In making the selection I have been guided by a desire to furnish the reader with the material necessary for an answer to the question, What was the secret of his power?

How is it?

"People sometimes say to me, 'How is it, Weaver, that the Lord blesses your labours so?'

"'Well, I don't know, except it is that I trust in God. There is nothing else. It depends upon what God does, and not upon what we do.'

"I sometimes say to my wife, 'Well, lass, I do not know how it is that people come to hear me, and how it is that the Lord blesses my labours.' And she says: 'You know you ask for it; you know you trust in the Lord; and that is how it is: for he that trusteth in the Lord shall never be confounded.'"

A Tremendous Power Somewhere.

"There is power in the Gospel. Sceptics may scoff and sneer, and say they will do this and that, but the

Gospel can stand against all the attacks of infidels and of devils too: it can and does save men from the burning gulf. Glory be to God! the Gospel of Christ can save to the very uttermost all that come unto God through Jesus.

"I am no astronomer. I look above and around me, and I see there is some mysterious power at work in the natural world; but I do not understand it. If I were to say that the sun went round the earth, the astronomer would call me an ignorant blockhead, and tell me the earth goes round the sun at the rate of many thousand miles a minute. I cannot understand how it is. I see that there must be a tremendous moving power somewhere; but I cannot tell where this moving power comes from, nor can the astronomer either.

"So with the waves of the ocean. As we stand upon the sea beach, and gaze upon the big waves that are rolling in one after another, dashing against the rocks, and making the vessels sailing on their bosom creak and tremble, we see there is a tremendous power somewhere; but where it comes from we cannot tell. I have stood by the side of a river and have seen the tide rising in the regular course quietly and slowly along its way; but presently the tide has rushed along and seemed to say, 'Stand back, for I am mightier than thou.' And the tide has rolled onwards with mighty power, but where the power was I could not tell.

"And in like manner, whilst I have stood by the black river that leads to hell, and its stream has swept numbers along upon its flood, I have looked; and, thank God, the mighty power of God has arrested them, and brought them back and I have heard the cry: 'God be merciful to me a sinner.' There is a power in the Gospel. It is *the power of the Living God.*"

To Thine own Self be True.

In the course of an address on "David and Goliath," Weaver said:

"Saul ordered his armour-bearer, 'Dress him in my armour.' Then David essayed to go; but he could not, for he had not proved them. Would to God that every preacher would prove himself. There are some who put on Mr. Wesley's armour; and some, Mr. Whitefield's; and some, Mr. Spurgeon's; and some that of other men. If you cannot fight in your own clothes, you cannot fight in another man's.

"As I travel about and see men doing this, I often wonder how they can put these men's old sermons before the people: we have read them all in bygone times. I would not give twopence for all the skeleton sermons in the world. If, instead of spending their time in getting off by heart the sermons of other men, they had spent the same amount of time on their knees, the Lord would have given them a power over men's hearts. May God pardon all who wear other men's armour.

"There is a separate suit for every one of the Lord's soldiers: for every one also there is a separate sword. May God help you to gird on your own. You cannot fight in Wesley's armour. He had his trim; Whitefield had his; Knox had his; and Richard Baxter had his. Where did these men get the power? In the closet. Paul had the power of God upon him; but he did not imitate Peter, or John, or James. In his own way he said, 'The Gospel is the power of God unto salvation.' Throw away all such imitations. Ask God to bless you with his power, and clothe you with his Spirit, and you will be enabled to do good in his Name."

Not Enough in Earnest.

"I would sooner have to do with the outcasts of society than with Gospel-hardened sinners. They go to God's house Sunday after Sunday, and they listen to God's word, but it never seems to move them. They say the man was 'a fluent preacher' or 'an intellectual preacher,' and that is all. I see large bills saying that a minister of the Gospel is going to give readings from 'The Old English Poets.' Our cry is, 'Escape for thy life: look not behind thee: remember Lot's wife.' Souls are going to hell, and ministers should be up and doing. They should not be idle six days of the week, and then stand up on Sunday and cry to the Sabbath-breaker to repent and take heed. Our cry is, 'Monday-breaker, Tuesday-breaker, Wednesday-breaker, Thursday-breaker, Friday-breaker, Saturday-breaker, six-days-a-week-breaker—repent and take heed!' If we believe that souls are going to hell, let us try to bring them to Christ. If one soul is of more value than ten thousand worlds, let us try to save that soul as a brand from the eternal burning. May the Lord help us to do it! We are not enough in earnest about souls; or else we should see the Lord's arm made bare, and souls flocking as doves to their windows."

IN THE SWELLING OF JORDAN—I. THE SCEPTIC.

"Infidelity is dark, dismal, dreadful. Listen to yonder dying sceptic. Death is coming, and it grows darker. 'Now for the grand secret. Dark! Dark!! Dark!!! I think I have been deceived. Oh, the waters are cold! Oh, what's that? The devil has seized me. What a fool I have been! I am going down the stairs into the eternal vaults. I hear the howling of the damned, and I see the flames of hell. Oh, that devilish infidelity! My feet are already in the flames! I am Lost! *Lost!* LOST!!'" (As Weaver uttered each of the last three words in our church he descended one step of the pulpit stair, striking it so heavily with his heel that the dull thud was a weird accompaniment to his despairing shriek "Lost!" It was awful.)

"Will you," he continued, "cry 'Fire! FIRE! FIRE!' to the sleeping inmates of a burning house, and shall not I shout 'Hell-fire! HELL-FIRE! HELL-FIRE!' to my brothers and my sisters who sleep upon the brink of everlasting woe? If you had stood by the death-beds I have stood by, and heard the dying shrieks of lost souls going down to the fiery lake of hell, you'd say, 'Richard, tell about it; they want to be warned.'

"Some people say, 'Talk to me about the joys of heaven as much as you've a mind to; but this preaching about hell unnerves me.' If you can't bear to hear about it, how will you bear to feel it? How many of you mothers are suckling your children for hell?

"There was a young man condemned at Chester, and

when the judge put on his black cap and sentenced him to be hanged by the neck till he was dead, his mother, who stood near, wrung her hands, and cried, 'Oh, my son! Oh, my son!' But the son turned upon her with 'Mother, you're the cause!' O mothers, think of that before it be too late."

In the Swelling of Jordan—II. The Believer.

"I remember a poor collier, who had his leg taken off by the conductors of a pit. The poor fellow was coming up the shaft, when his leg was caught, cut off, and fell to the bottom. I shall never forget that scene. He said he felt he had got his death-blow. Oh, how he rejoiced in the prospect of heaven! He said to me:

"'Richard, if I can but see my dear wife, I shall be satisfied.'

"Just as we were removing him, his wife came, for she had heard of the accident. Her first words were:

"'Is he alive?'

"I said to her, 'He is alive.'

"And she joyfully exclaimed, 'Thank God. If he can only speak to me, I shall be satisfied.'

"The doctor was trying to stop the bleeding, but he could not; and we could see that the paleness of death was coming over him. The wife kissed him—the face dirty as it was—it was the farewell kiss of affection. He assured her that all was well in the swelling of Jordan. And then the daughter came from the factory to see him die. They were certain that all would be right on the other side of Jordan. And the dying man, did he grieve? No. He asked his dear wife to hold his hand while Jesus received his soul.

"'Bless thee, lass,' said he, 'the Lord will be a father to our children—the Lord bless thee. Give me our child, and let me kiss it.' And as he put his poor dying arm round the little babe, which smiled at him, he said, 'The Lord bless thee.' The group gathered round, and he said—

> Lend, lend your wings, I mount, I fly,
> O grave, where is thy victory!
> O death, where is thy sting!

"And he said to me, 'Richard, I am going to my farewell sleep, and willingly lay aside my pit clogs, and am ready to welcome heaven.' Such was the end of a Christian life."

A New Creation.

"I made lots of resolutions for five-and-twenty years that I would turn over a fresh leaf, but I made every one in the strength of Richard Weaver. And how many times I have wept in private, and actually knelt down and said a form of prayer before God that I would begin to do different! Those iniquities and crimes that I had committed rose up against me, and I was determined to turn over a fresh leaf; but old companions and the world were so closely bound to me, that I could not say this thing and the other to them. But as soon as ever I got a peep at Christ, that moment I had no desire for public-houses or public-house companions. As soon as ever I got a sight of Christ, that moment I could say, 'I am a new creature in Christ Jesus? Old things have passed away, and all things have become new.'

"You that say, 'I wish I was as happy as the man standing speaking to us to-night,' you see before you only a reformed drunkard, who was not reformed by teetotalism, but by the grace of God.

"You might sign a temperance pledge, and be very good, moral, kind, benevolent, and charitable, and become a good citizen and neighbour. You might become a good father, a good son, a good mother, a good daughter; but that is not all. You know you have to pass through the river that we have just been singing of, and then how will it be with you? Will you say to the people around your dying couch, 'Fetch me the pledge, and hang it by the side of my dying bed?'"

ADOPTED.

"Suppose you and I were next-door neighbours. A poor little starving boy, with neither shoes nor stockings on his feet, comes to my door some cold winter morning, and knocks at it. We will suppose that I have never known what it is to be a father, and therefore speak to the boy with less kindly tone than I would to the dog at my feet, as I ask, 'Where do you come from?'

"'I have no home,' says the poor boy.

"'Be off with you. There is a workhouse for you. Go there.'

"Then he goes to the door of your house, and knocks there. You had some little children once; but they passed away from you, and your heart is not so hard to the poor boy at the door as mine was. You feel tears running down your cheek, and you say:

"'Where do you come from?'

"'Why, sir,' he says, 'I have to lie under hedges, and in carts, and wherever I can.'

"'Where is your mother?'

"'I have none; she is dead.'

"'Where is your father?'

"'He is dead, too, sir.'

"There is a spring of true sympathy somewhere in your heart, and you go to your wife and say, 'Well, lass, come and look at the little starving boy at the door.' She looks at him, and sees his feet bleeding from being cut with the stones, and the sight goes to her heart; and she thinks:

"'Ah, if he were a child of mine, he should never be in that fix!'

"'Well, dear,' you ask, 'what do you say now? Will you take him and adopt him as your own?'

"'Yes,' says the good woman, 'we will.'

"'Very well.'

"'Now, my boy,' you say, 'if you will comply with our rules and regulations, we will take you and bring you up as our own child.'

"The wife clothes him with the clothes of her poor dead child, and puts its shoes upon his feet, and feeds him. The next Sabbath day you all go to the same church together, and I come alongside of you and say, 'That is not your child, is it, neighbour?'

"'Yes, it is,' say you.

"But I am not convinced, and I say to the boy: 'My boy, are you not the lad that came to my door begging?'

"'Yes,' is the answer.

"'Do you *know* that you are an adopted child?'

"'To be sure. Don't you think I know the difference between being then cold and now warm?—between being then hungry and now fed?—between being then ragged and now clothed? To be sure I do. You cannot persuade me that I am not an adopted child.'

"Dear friends, Jesus Christ found me a poor beggar on the way to hell. Glory be to God! His kindness did not end with shedding a tear over me: He *took me in*, and clothed me, and fed me. Bless the Lord! I know in whom I believe. Pardoned sinners must know it, because 'He that believeth on the Son of God hath the witness in himself.' What a blessing is that! If I did not believe that, I would never speak to sinners again."

Cleanliness, one of the Fruits.

"If a woman tells me she is converted, and I enter into her house, and find it filthy, I would not believe about the conversion. If a mother says she is converted, and she has dirty children and dirty clothes, I would not believe it. Therefore when beggars come to beg of me, I tell them, if they are dirty, they must go and wash before I can give them anything. And so if there are any of you that have dirty homes, and I come to visit you, and you profess to be Christians, I should not be against telling you that you do not know Christ, because that is not the fruit of it."

Desire for Unity, another of the Fruits.

"A man at Leek got converted, and on one occasion when I went into his dressing-room, for he was a dear friend of mine, I saw, in a little drawer of the dressing-table, his precious treasure of gems. He said, 'This is my drawer of jewels.' So I began to peep into it, and the thought arose in my mind, 'I wonder how many drawers of jewels the Lord has got.'

"There is the Church of England drawer, and there are as good Church people as Dissenters; there are jewels there as well as hypocrites and counterfeits. Then there is the Independent drawer, and the Lord has got a number of jewels there. Then there is the Baptist drawer with a lot of little jewels, and a good big one, that shines yonder at London, called Spurgeon! and if you search you will find another drawer full of Wesleyan gems, and still another called Reformers.

"Dear me, what a lot of sects and drawers! I would to God that the bottom would drop out, and that the whole chest might become one big drawer! Such a lot of drawers, and sects, and parties, fairly puzzles some people, who wonder how it is, seeing that all Christians are children of one common Father. Oh, may the time soon come when Christ shall be the drawer to hold us all! The Lord help us to strive after it!"

A FORGIVING SPIRIT, ANOTHER OF THE FRUITS.

"A poor prodigal, at a place where I was speaking one night, said to me, 'I came, sir, not to hear you preach, but to put my hands into other people's pockets; I came to thieve, but I stopped to pray.' He rose from his knees a saved man. 'How do you know?' some people may say. Well, I will put it in this way—he professed to be saved. If a man, by continual consistent conduct, proves the truth of what he professes, I have a right to believe him. It is over five years since, and he is walking upright before God now; and I believe five years is enough to test whether a person is on the Lord's side or not.

"The brother who prayed with him said to the young man, 'You were brought up in the same class that I was, in such a place, were you not?'

"'Yes,' was the answer.

"'Do you know So-and-so?'

"'I do.'

"'Are you not So-and-so's prodigal?'

"'I am.'

"'Don't weep, then; but come to my house, I have a spare bed, and you shall go thither.'

"Accordingly, we all three got into a cab together. Presently the young man said:

"'I should like to call on my father and mother, and tell them what has happened to me, and ask my father's forgiveness. I am unworthy to enter his house, but I should like to go and tell him.'

"We drove up to his house, and sat in the cab while he went to the door. A servant girl opened it, and I could see some more people in the lobby.

"'Is my father in?'

"'Yes.'

"She brought the old man to the door, and there was the little daughter, and the mother, wiping the tears from her eyes. The young man dropped on his knees, saying:

"'Father, God has forgiven me to-night: will you forgive me?—for He has pardoned all my sins.'

"'Oh,' said the little sister, 'there's my brother John!'"

"But the father turned away, telling him: 'You must come again in three weeks; then we will see how it is with you. Good night!'

"So he came away; and at the friend's house he was too sorrowful to eat, but he sat down and wept:

"'Oh, Mr. Weaver, did you hear it? It was not what my father said that affected me so much—I deserved all that; but did you hear my little sister cry: "There's my brother"? That affects me most. She acknowledged me as her brother, did she not?'

"We tried to comfort him, but he cried: 'I deserve it all, I deserve it all!'

"Soon there was a knock at the door, and a servant girl was introduced. She said to the young man: 'You must come home, sir; your father has sent me to fetch you.'

"'How is it that he has forgiven me so soon?'

"'We had family worship,' the girl said. 'Master read the Bible, and then he prayed, and when he came to that part of the Lord's prayer, "Forgive us our trespasses, as we forgive them that trespass against us," the little girl said: "Stop, father!" "Why, my dear?" "You have not forgiven my brother." Master could get no further, and he sent me to fetch you home.'"

The Lost Sheep.

"Wasn't it just natural that the man should care more about his one lost sheep than about the ninety-nine that hadn't strayed away? Here's a farmer owns a hundred sheep. Well, at night he counts 'em, and he makes one short. He goes over them again; perhaps he's reckoned wrong. No; it's only ninety-nine again. He goes in to his wife, who is sitting by the kitchen fire, waiting till he comes to supper—'Why, lass, there's one gone. Poor thing, he must have got over the wall.' (Ah! the devil's always ready to help a poor sheep of Christ's over the wall.) He starts in search of him. By-and-by he sees the footmarks—ah, thither he is! But now he has to mind where he treads; he has to make a spring now and then over some boggy place, and the land is all sopping wet. But he sees the track of the wanderer, and now he hears, 'Ba-a,' and the great soft eyes of the creature stare up at him from a quagmire, as if to say, 'Oh, master, help me out.' He takes him up, and puts him over his shoulders, and the black mud drips down his jacket; but he doesn't mind that. At last he comes to the brook that skirts his orchard, and there he washes all the filth away; and the poor thing trots into the fold with such a happy bleat, as if to say, 'Thank you, sir.' Now, that's how Jesus fetches back his wanderer. Only He doesn't put him across his shoulders; He puts him in his bosom, and then He takes and washes him in the fountain opened for sin and for uncleanness, the fountain filled with his own precious blood. That's what He did for me many years ago."

The Woman that Touched Jesus.

"I imagine I see a little boy tripping up the street of a certain town, singing, 'Hosanna to the Son of David!' A poor afflicted woman stands on her doorstep and hears the child. 'What is that you say?' she asks, as he is passing by her house. 'Oh,' says he, 'haven't you heard about Jesus of Nazareth? He's cured blind Bartimeus that used to sit at the wayside begging; and He has raised a young man to life that was being carried to his grave; and healed ten lepers all at once; and the people that have sick relations bring them and lay them at his feet, and He cures them all. And those who have no friends to bring them, if they can only just touch Him, are made perfectly whole. 'Oh,' cries the poor woman, 'if that's true, He can cure my disease that I've been tormented with these twelve years. When will He be here, my little man?' 'Why,' says the child, 'He'll be here directly. He's coming this way. There! don't you hear the noise of the multitude? Look! here they come. Hosanna! hosanna to the Son of David!' and away goes the little boy to tell his mother that the Prophet she has taught him to look for is come at last. 'Well, I'll go,' says the poor thing, timidly. 'I'll get behind Him. Maybe He won't pity me; but that dear little lad said as many as touched Him were made whole: I'll go and try, however.'

"I imagine I see the poor, weak creature, who has spent all her living on physicians that only made her worse, drawing her tattered shawl around her and wriggling her way through the crowd. They push her aside, but she says, 'I'll try again.' She winds to the right, then to the left; now nearer, and the next minute farther off than ever. But still she perseveres, although she seems to have so little chance of getting through the throng, which is thickest round the Man she wants. Well done, poor woman! Try again; it's for your life, you know. That disease will be your death, if you don't get it cured; and a touch of his clothes will do it. I imagine I hear one rudely asking the fainting creature, 'Where are you pushing to? You've no business here.' 'Ah,' she answers, 'I see there a Man whose like I never saw before. Let me but touch his garment, and I shall be as well as any of you.' And now another step or two, and she can hear his gentle voice speaking kindly to Jairus, as He walks home with him to heal his little daughter lying at the point of death. The woman stretches out her hand, but she isn't near enough. Another step—yes, now she touches—it is but the hem of his garment; but it is all she needs. Glory to Jesus! her issue of blood is dried, and immediately she feels in her body that she is healed. Glory to Jesus! she touched, and was made perfectly whole. And if there was virtue in his garment, isn't there efficacy in his blood? May God help you to come to Christ to-night."

WELCOME HOME.

While conducting the missions that he held in our church, Weaver sang the following hymn as a solo more frequently than he sang any other:

> O sinner, come to Jesus;
>   No longer roam;
> He waits from sin to free us,
>   Oh come, then, quickly come.
> He'll meet you at his gate,
> And will make your heart rejoice,
> If you'll follow in his footsteps,
> And listen to his voice,
> Making music in the ear,
> Amidst sin's deep midnight gloom:
>   O sinner, He has loved you,
>   Welcome, welcome home.

Welcome Home.

O sinner, come then quickly,
 Obey his gracious call,
And Christ will on you brightly
 Cause light and joy to fall:
Soon, soon your course may end,
And the day of grace be past,
When with tears, and grief, and wailing,
You will find your fate is cast;
But He listens for your voice,
And He longs to see you come;
  O sinner, He has loved you,
   Welcome, welcome home.

Our days are sad without Him,
 And night is long and drear;
Then open thy heart to Him,
 Cry, " Welcome, Jesus, here."
Thy pathway He has watched,
And has often cast a ray
To guide thy erring footsteps
In the true and living way;
But his heart was grieved again,
When He found you would not come:
  O sinner, He has loved you,
   Welcome, welcome home.

XIV.

From the Soldier's Letter-bag.

IT is exceedingly difficult to get a perfectly natural portrait. Artist and sitter conspire to yield to the temptation to introduce "pose." Of course, the artist does his best to give the "pose" the appearance of absence of "pose." His highest art is to conceal art. But the "pose" is there all the same. A similar temptation besets the biographer. A perfectly natural biographical portrait is seldom seen. Conscious of the force of this current, I gladly avail myself of the opportunity of allowing Weaver to be seen where no "pose" was possible. His letters to his wife and daughters were not written under the consciousness that the public were looking on. They are evidence that he was in no way different in private from what he was in public. They prove that there was no "pose" about Weaver. If he appeared to the public to be an evangelist, it was because he was at heart an evangelist. The following are extracts from letters to his wife:

Dorking, March 11th, 1885.

Many of the people who come to the meetings come as far as six and seven miles. Last night a mother and two daughters came five miles. The mother had heard me twenty years ago, and had got saved; and she thought if she could get her grown-up daughters to hear me, they would be saved also. It was as the mother wished and believed. They both professed to have found the Lord. Mother and daughters went home happy. Praise the Lord!

Wimbledon, April 3rd, 1885.

Twelve months to-day we were made one before the Lord. It has been twelve months of affliction to me, and of trial to you; but we could not see these beforehand. It is a sore burden to me that I should have brought on *you* these trials and burdens that I have. I thought it would have been different with us in money matters from what it has been; but we must cast all our care upon the Lord. Do you ever take notice how much it takes to keep the house? We shall have to sacrifice each other's company at present, as you see we can hardly make ends meet. It is hard for me to be away from home; but I cannot forget what the Lord sacrificed for me. We shall have to take another house with less rent. Cheer up: it will be better by-and-by. The Lord bless you, my dear wife!

After lamenting the disappointment he experienced in meeting so many who had the profession without the reality, in a letter dated Portsmouth, May 3rd, 1885, he thus breaks out:

My dear wife, and children, and niece,—Let us have a real Christ, whatever others have. My prayer to God is that my family all may be real Christians, filled with the love of Christ; and not afraid to let others know it, and not unwilling to live simply to bring others to Him. I hope Frank will give himself to the Lord and work for Him.

Belfast, June 15th, 1885.

I had a warm reception here. People may say what they like about the Irish, but they are so warm-hearted that they seemed ready to eat me.

Belfast, June 19th, 1885.

I hope you will have a good day on Sunday, and that you will all get a big lift heavenward and get a baptism of the Holy Ghost. Let us all try and live more like Jesus, and come out more from the world, and get more filled with the love of God; and then we all will enjoy Christ more. The Lord wants us to be out and out for Him. He does not want us to be dwarfs. He wants us to be giants in his cause.

Belfast, June 29th, 1886.

I want Reggie and Bewley to give their minds to reading more than they do.

Cambridge, 1893.

This is the hardest place I was ever in. I have no after-meetings. I just speak and close the meeting, and leave them with the Lord.

London, 1893.

I hope the Lord will give me strength to hold up for this mission. I do want to be able to go to the Scotch church, if the Lord will.

The following are extracts from letters to his son Reginald:

Barrow-in-Furness, 1882.

You will be glad to hear that last night as I was concluding speaking they began to cry out for pardon and mercy, and came rushing out of the gallery and the body of the chapel—men and women—to the communion rails. Praise the Lord! The Lord is with us. Pray on, Reggie, for the Lord to save sinners. I know my children will be glad to hear that the Lord is using their father in bringing souls to Christ.

Portsmouth, 1885.

There are lots of openings for young men who feel called of God to preach the old gospel of Christ. It does my soul good to see how the Lord is leading my dear boys. Your own dear mother, if alive, would have been glad; but I don't doubt but what she knows all about it; give your mind to study and reading.

This extract is from a letter to his daughters, Bessie and Hettie:

Sale, September 2nd, 1884.

Now my dear daughters, I hope you are loving and looking to Jesus, and praying to Him to make you his followers. I want you to grow up to try and be as much like Jesus as you can be;

for He is the only One to imitate. I am praying that you grow up in the fear of the Lord, to be like Mary and Martha. Read John xi. 5, and think over what is said: and take it to yourselves, and remember that He loves you also, and read it thus: "Now Jesus loves Bessie and Hettie and their brothers." The Lord bless you, my dear daughters, and make and keep you both good, dear children of the Lord.

The following extracts are from his letters to his youngest daughter:—

London, November 8th, 1895.

My dear daughter Hettie,—I was glad to get your letter, and to hear you were going to play now. There are two daughters here just about as old as you and Bessie. They put me in mind of you.

I hope, my dear child, you will give your mind to study. Try to be a good girl, and look to Jesus for help. I think I have read of a little girl that did her lessons better because she asked the Lord to help her. You can read in the 14th chapter of John, and see what the Lord says on that. He is willing to help those that ask Him. It's nice to have the Lord to help us in all things. We can ask Him to help us to love Him, and to be like Jesus. Try to be like Him, dear child. Do what your mother wants you. You know she will do anything for you. Had your own mother lived, she would have liked you to love and fear the Lord Jesus, and to read your Bible and other good books. What a comfort it is to know that Christ Jesus, who loved you and gave Himself for you, is yours. To have the blessing of the Lord, my dear child, is worth more than all the money in the world. The riches of the world often bring a curse; but where Christ is there is love, and peace, and joy, and pardon, here; and when we have done with the world—heaven. The Lord bless you, my dear child!

Fifeshire, July 4th, 1892.

My dear daughter Hettie,—I write a letter to you that you will get on your twenty-first birthday, and I pray that the Lord will bless you with fresh blessing from his Loving Self, as He who loved you and gave Himself for you. What a comfort and blessing to know that Christ is yours! I pray that you may get fresh strength from Him, to live nearer to, and be more like Him;

to confess Him to others; and to let people know you belong to Christ, and are not ashamed of Him. May the Lord bless you, my dear child, with grace and love! Your own mother used to pray, "Lord, make us *Bible* Christians," and I pray the same. The longer I live the more I can see a deal of sham profession. Let me advise you to get your Bible, and study about the blood, and you will see you get sheltered under the blood, and every other blessing you get is through the blood.

The following is one of the last letters Weaver wrote. It was written to one of his converts, Harry Wintle, the son of Richard's attached friend, Mr. Thomas Wintle, Hon. Supt. of the Undenominational Christian Mission and Ragged Schools, Pontymoile, etc., South Wales.

Moss Bank, Alderley Edge, Cheshire, Feb. 15, 1896.

Dear Harry,—I was so glad to get your letter; it's very kind of you to think of me. I do pray that you may grow in grace as you grow in years, and be a comfort to your parents and a light to the other boys at the Mission. You see I have not been able to leave my house since I left you. I felt very ill then, and I have thought sometimes I was going Home.

It is sad about the poor men in the Rhondda Valley explosion: it teaches us to be ready. I don't doubt but many of them heard me preach when I was in the Valley a few years ago; and if they were prepared and saved through His blood, they are now singing before King Jesus. That's better than singing before the Queen!

Give my love to all the old men and women, the young men and maidens, and the boys and girls, at the Mission Hall, and ask them to keep on praying for me, for I pray for them and you every day, that the Lord will bless and keep all looking to Jesus. Give my love to your dear mother, father, and sister, and to all at Bethany House. The Lord be with you, my little friend Harry; and I want you, if you are spared to your parents, to be a comfort to them both. The Lord bless you and watch over you is my prayer.

I doubt if I ever shall be able to come and see you again. Peace be with you.

Yours ever in Jesus,
RICHARD WEAVER.

And almost from within sight of the pearly gates, one hour before his home-going, he sent the following telegram to Mr. Wintle, "Just going home shouting Victory."

On turning to the

LETTERS RECEIVED BY WEAVER,

I find it exceedingly difficult to make a selection. It is only a selection that has been put into my hands, and yet the bundle is so large that the letters in it would themselves fill a goodly-sized volume. I have read them all. As I read, I was taken by Bunyan's Interpreter "behind the wall, where I saw a man with a vessel of oil in his hand, of the which he did also continually cast (but secretly) into the fire."

The Good Shepherd knows that the faith of his tried ones requires special sustenance. Richard had his special trials; but in these letters there is of heavenly sustenance enough and to spare.

If Weaver, as an evangelist, could in any sense be said to have had an earthly employer, that employer was the late Reginald Radcliffe. Did the employé satisfy his employer with regard to work? Let the following letter from Radcliffe answer.

Hampstead, January 7th, 1861.

My dear Weaver,—Do not be in a hurry to work. Always bear in mind it is not a few battles we have to fight, but a day-after-day work; therefore, do take care. I hear that one of the two men who were so greatly used in the Welsh Revival is now laid by with something like weakness of mind. Do breathe awhile. The first thing for you now is to try and rest and get back your health. I did not like that shudder you had, and do think you must have a good rest. You know how you are wanted at Bristol and perhaps we could both go together as far as Bristol, and I could penetrate further, and still be a door-opener for you; and if afterwards my beloved brother comes and takes my congregations, and runs away with my friends, let God be glorified.

Lovingly yours as ever,
REGINALD RADCLIFFE.

The following, which in the original is entirely independent of capital I's or of ordinary rules of spelling or grammar, is one of the most touching of all.

Macclesfield, January 21st, 1861.

Dear Richard Weaver,—You are beginning to touch the publican's feelings. One, I know, has already said you have been the means of two or three of her best customers leaving; and if you stop much longer, she may shut up. It would have been better for me had they shut up years ago, although two of my brothers are in the trade. Yours—one who has listened to you this last week, and found much benefit. God bless you; and may He protect you when far away from home. May Heaven bless you!

Alongside of that communication from some unlettered brother, let me put the following extract from a letter written by Lord Carrick:

You will remember our meeting at Oldham some years ago, *when beloved Harry Moorhouse and I were there born to an inheritance reserved for us* who are kept for it. And that grace which brought us salvation and is sufficient for us on our pilgrimage journey will bring us full blessing in glory when our Lord comes. Nothing but failure down here, but no failure with Him; for He is able. The Lord will bless and sustain you.

Ever yours in our Lord,
CARRICK.

The following is from a student:

Glasgow, July 20th, 1876.

My dear spiritual Father,—It was with tears I read your letter to Brother Hill, the evangelist, whom I asked if he could tell me anything about you. There are thousands in Glasgow who are praying for you, and who love you with all the warmth of Christian affection. You ask who thus writes. Well, I am a Yorkshireman; but I was in Glasgow when you were here. Then I was hastening on post haste to hell. You, by God's help, stopped me in my mad career. Ever since I have been preaching Jesus. For nine years I have been a missionary, and am now a student in the Glasgow University.

Glasgow, 1886.

Dear Brother in Christ,—I enclose two copies of a Gaelic translation of the hymn, "Be in time," from your hymn-book. The translation was done by Mrs. McKellar, one of the best of Gaelic-speaking poetesses. It appeared shortly after the Revival in Scotland. It was a great favourite, and moved many to tears. The Day alone will declare the good it has been the means of doing.

Yours,

NEIL CAMPBELL.

Canterbury (no date).

Dear Sir,—Many years have passed since the Lord put it into my heart to hear you preach at Vernon Chapel, King's Cross. I shall never forget that night. The first hymn given out was "My Jesus, I love Thee." Although that arrested my attention, it was the text which the Lord sent right home to my heart. It has been there ever since. The words were, "How shall we escape, if we neglect so great salvation?" My sins stared me in the face; but before the service concluded, I saw Him through whom salvation came. Oh, sir, I was happy! so happy, I scarcely knew how to contain myself. I have never ceased to love you as the instrument through whom the Lord made Himself known to me. It is this love which has prompted me to write to you and tell you that your labour that night was not in vain. I heard of your trouble in the shape of slander. My heart was stirred within me, and I wished to publish that you were my spiritual father, and that your work was a real work. I can assure you, dear sir, that although all men were to be against you, I should still be for you.

With Christian love,

I am, &c.,

JOHN WHITCOMBE.

Amongst the messages of sympathy I notice letters from Lord Cairns; Mr. Stoughton, of Hodder and Stoughton; Mr. Wm. Jones, of Bangor; Dr. Hagart, Santhal Mission; a Russian sister in Florence; Miss C. Balfour, of Lowestoft; and from many others. The burden of the comfort of which they all speak is well given in the following extract from a letter written by Von Schulthess-Rechberg of Zurich.

> The Lord thy Shepherd is! dread not, nor be dismayed;
> He leads thee on through thorny paths by ways his hand hath made;
> The stormiest wind He rules, the wildest wave He binds!
> Thou hast "the secret of the stairs," for to his heart it winds;
> Green pastures wait for thee, and when thou needest rest
> Beside the softly flowing stream, He'll bear thee on his breast.
> Trust Him whate'er betide, on Him cast all thy care;
> The wilderness has pleasant spots, and He will guide thee there.
> Oh, watch we by the way! the Bridegroom soon shall come,
> And the silver trumpet's joyful shout shall call his loved ones home;
> Oh, watch we by the way, and all his footsteps trace;
> Keep close beside Him, hear his voice: we soon shall see his face.

I put in the following extracts from a letter, written by Dr. Barnardo, as evidence that in addition to the miles of shadow in Weaver's pathway there were not wanting furlongs of sunshine:—

18 to 26, Stepney Causeway, London, E.
April 7th, 1884.

My dear Richard,—I had your letter, and I had a good laugh over it. I am glad you have got a good wife as quiet as yourself. If she is not a good deal quieter, I pity the house that has you both in lodgings. My dear friend, you may be sure you have our very warm and hearty congratulations.

However, we must not let you go to sleep, or else you will be getting too fat; and that would never do. I want you and Mrs.

Weaver to come up to London for Easter. We will have your two rooms at the Edinboro' Castle made very nice for the young bride and bridegroom, so be sure you both come.

I must tell you that Easter holidays are great times in the East of London; numbers of people think of nothing but pleasure, dissipation, and sin; and it is most important that at that time we should hold up some strong attraction to draw them aside from the perils of their position. As I knew on getting your letter this morning that you would come, I went up at once and announced you in *The Christian*; so that it will be published on Thursday.

But amongst all his letters none was so prized by Weaver as the following from the late C. H. Spurgeon. I understand it is the last letter Mr. Spurgeon wrote before he left England *en route* for heaven:—

Westwood, Beulah Hill, Upper Norwood,
October 23rd, 1891.

Dear Friend,—Thank you much. I too have had a weak heart so as to be compelled to be carried upstairs to bed by two men. *That* is getting better. You must feel it a great hindrance and trial. I am not free from my disease yet; but it waxes weaker and weaker and will be driven out. God is good indeed.

May you have many souls at your last service at the Castle. Oh that they may fly like doves to their windows, freely, numerously, at once. Tell them I KNOW HOW SURE A SUPPORT JESUS IS WHEN WE ARE IN THE FACE OF DEATH. FAITH IN HIM REDUCES DYING TO SLEEPING, AND MAKES PAIN ITSELF INTO A BASS NOTE IN THE PERFECT MUSIC OF DELIGHT IN GOD.

May you be strengthened to bear clear testimony to the power of faith! May your own soul be full of joy and peace through believing!

We leave, myself and wife, on Monday early,

Yours in Christ Jesus,
C. H. SPURGEON.

XV.

Honourable Discharge.

IN my introductory personal reminiscences of the evangelist, I have made mention of the fact that when he conducted the two missions in White Memorial Free Church, he stayed in our home. He could not hide his heart-hunger for something that was withheld from him. The Lord was blessing him wonderfully in the church; night after night was witnessing a marvellous outpouring of the spirit of "repentance and forgiveness of sins"; and yet the happiness of the evangelist was lacking in completeness.

When at last he gave me the key to the door of his heart, I discovered what it was for which he was yearning. He greatly desired before he left the battlefield to have the joy of standing once more shoulder to shoulder with his old comrades in the fight. Ere he left Glasgow, the prayer of his heart was granted. He had gone from us to conduct a mission in St. George's Cross Tabernacle. About ten days after leaving us he called at our home. He did not need to tell me that something had happened to him that filled his heart with gladness. It shone from his face. He had gone to a mid-afternoon meeting on the previous day. On leaving that meeting, he and his old comrade, the

Rev. Robert Howie, of Free St. Mary's, Govan, suddenly found themselves face to face. That seemingly accidental meeting led of course to the usual inquiries after each other's welfare. These in their turn led to an invitation to Weaver to call on Mr. Howie at his manse. The acceptance of that led to an appeal from Mr. Howie to Weaver to conduct an evangelistic mission in his church. With exceeding readiness Richard promised to do so. Mr. Howie is deservedly held in esteem in church circles in Scotland. The news spread that he was having Weaver. The lead of the Convener of the Home Mission Committee of the Free Church was followed. Requests for Weaver's services were received in such abundance, even before he left Glasgow, that it seemed as if it would be wise for him to flit his home to our city forthwith. He was seriously contemplating such a move when he left for the South to fulfil a promise to conduct a mission in Pontymoile, South Wales.

The time appointed for the St. Mary's Mission drew on. The bills were on the hoardings. The morning had come on which he was to start for Mr. Howie's. But he was in the grip of his old trouble—bodily prostration. The doctor forbade him leaving his room. He had to send a telegram announcing his inability. It was a sore disappointment to his friends here. Their disappointment was slight in comparison with his. But he meekly said: "The will of the Lord be done!" He hoped that the Mission in Free St. Mary's might be arranged for at some not distant date. It was so arranged; but it was not to be. His last mission had been conducted. One more conflict, and the wars of the veteran would be over.

The Easter of 1896 was drawing on. On the Tuesday preceding that anniversary of our Lord's Resurrection, Weaver caught a chill that sent him to his bed. No immediate danger was feared by those around him. He himself, however, seems to have been aware that already he was FOOT TO FOOT WITH THE LAST ENEMY. As they helped him up the stairs, he told them he would not come down again until he was carried down in his coffin. Thursday saw a great change. It was evident that death was in the cup. For him it had no terrors. He was capable of playful humour while setting his house in order.

As an instance of this, I may mention his manner of giving instructions about the disposal of his books. He had gathered a large library. He told his sons that they were to divide his books among themselves, giving the one with the least brains the largest share of the books! He left them to settle who was who for themselves. After awhile he grimly smiled and said:

"After all, it won't do. It will not make you equal. You may surround a man with books as you like: unless he has brains to take them in, they are no good to him."

Early on Saturday morning he had a further relapse. In the evening it was seen that the end was not far off. All his family were gathered round him except his eldest daughter, Mrs. Hardwicke. She was detained through the illness of her child.

On Saturday evening he could speak only with the greatest difficulty. One of his sons prayed with him, and after that he began to speak with great unction and with wonderful voice.

He gave the following instructions with regard to his burial:

"If you sing at my funeral, let it be the hymn:—

> In evil long I took delight,
>   Unawed by shame or fear;
> Till a new object met my sight,
>   And stopped my wild career.
> Oh, the Lamb, the bleeding Lamb!

If you put anything on my tombstone let it be, 'A great sinner saved by great grace.'"

To Bewley and Frank, his evangelist sons, he said:

"Many young men imitate great preachers; but one talent used for Christ is worth a thousand imitations."

"God's Word! You surely won't doubt that."

"Stick to Christ. Stick to the Cross."

"Live for heaven. Live for souls."

While his wife and children waited weeping on the bank, the pilgrim for whom the call had come entered the much-feared river. His exclamations told them how it fared with him in his struggle through the dark waters. Now it was the shout of triumph:

"Victory through the blood of the Lamb!"

Anon he was speaking of the
"Peace that passeth all understanding."
"Peace flowing like a river."

By-and-by they heard him say:
"Now I have found the ground."
"On Christ the solid rock I stand."
"I can do nothing but trust."

He kept pressing onward, and he was cheered with a vision of the end of the journey:

"My prize is in view."

"Easter Sunday with the Lord."

"I shall drink at the fountain."

After this he suffered most acutely. His breathing was agonizing to hear. Asked if he had much pain, he replied:

"It's only old nature struggling."

He was quite conscious till within three minutes of the end. But his soul was so far across the river that it was only in whispers that his voice reached the ears of the friends that he had left on the bank. He evidently longed for rest. His whispers were:

"Home." "Home." "Not far now."

Two hours before his departure he said:

"Let me lie down."

"The chariot wheels are rattling."

"It will soon be here."

An hour later he whispered:

"There's a light in the valley."

It proved the light of the longed-for chariot. At 11.20 he was taken with one of the fits which troubled him so much twenty-five years before. He had not had one for twenty years. The paroxysm was soon over, and there was a glorious calm. Writing at the time, of that last moment, Bewley says, "I have stood by dozens of death-beds, but never have I seen such a beautiful expression. He fell back on my arm and was gone."

Human eye hath not seen, nor hath human ear heard,

the full story of the glory that "the great change" brought to Richard Weaver. He had been wont to delight in a characteristic description of the contrast between the death of the sceptic and the death of the Christian. In the course of his address on the prayer— "Let me die the death of the righteous"—he summarized that contrast into four pregnant sentences:— "Now for a step into the dark," says the sceptic; "Now for a step into the light," says the Christian; "I am leaving all behind," says the sceptic; "I am going now to possess," says the Christian. His step into the light had been taken. He had entered on the possession of the incorruptible inheritance. There was no occasion to sorrow over him as over one who had given no promise of future usefulness.

But a chair was vacant at the fireside. A cheery companion had left the family circle. His incoming would be expected, and he would not appear. His voice would be listened for, and it would not again be heard. A great bereavement had been allowed. The gentle Jesus has, however, his own way of soothing the pain. Letters of sympathy came flocking from the four winds to Moss Bank, as doves to their windows. They came in such abundance that they compelled the bereaved to think of the good purpose to which the life just closed had been put. And if there was sorrow, keen and poignant, there was also thanksgiving, sincere and deep. The greater number of those messages of sympathy have been put into my hands. On reading them I am impressed with the evidence they afford that Weaver had been made of God a spiritual benefactor to representatives of every class. I am impressed also with the largeness of the number of the towns and villages in which are the homes of personal friends of "The Converted Collier." That bundle of letters is an evidence of something so unique that I am inclined to give the names and addresses. But "Directories" are of local rather than of general interest, so I forbear. He who wept at the grave of Lazarus has them in His book, and He may be trusted to redeem the pledge He gave in the following words:

"For whosoever shall give you a cup of water to drink in My name, because ye belong to Christ, verily I say unto you, he shall not lose his reward."

XVI.
Wreaths for the Warrior's Coffin.

IN Mosaic jurisprudence it was deemed imperative, in the more serious cases, to have the evidence of more than one witness. Many are the witnesses that are willing to give evidence as to the greatness of the blessing that Weaver was to his generation. Want of space compels me to be satisfied with the testimonies that follow.

FROM A FREE CHURCH COLLEGE PRINCIPAL.

The following testimony is from the pen of the late Rev. Principal Brown, D.D., of Aberdeen, who, at the advanced age of ninety-four, and within a few days of his decease, remembered distinctly the marvellous work of grace of thirty years ago.

"I had heard a good deal of Richard Weaver, the converted collier, and I expected much from him when he came to Aberdeen in the year 1864. I had a good opportunity of judging of the impression which he produced, as I was on the platform of the Music Hall with him every evening while he was here. I was the only minister of any denomination who was there, or even in the Hall. The numbers were not many at first; but before he left there was hardly standing room, and the Music Hall when packed holds three thousand. One who was present told me afterwards that he came there to make sport of Richard Weaver; but two lines of a hymn arrested his attention:

> His blood can make the foulest clean,
> His blood availed for me.

"'If there's a *foulest* upon earth, I am that man,' said he to himself; 'and if it can make me clean, it must be wonderful blood.' He could not leave the meeting; and that night was the turning-point of his life.

"The hymns, the prayers, and the preaching, were all in the same strain. The precious, cleansing blood of Christ was his constant theme, and he put the whole energy of his being into it. I have seen the veins swell on his temples, and his face suffuse with colour, from the pressure of his earnestness, as he bent over the platform swinging his arms while preaching or singing of the love of Christ. He had a voice powerful, yet sweet and full of tenderness, and far-reaching. He said himself he could make it heard by an audience of ten thousand, and I did not doubt it.

"One of his favourite hymns,

> Oh, the Lamb, the bleeding Lamb!

made a deep impression. A young man told me of his conversion through that hymn. He had gone, unconverted, with a friend, to a social gathering of young men. The talk turned chiefly on Richard Weaver and his meetings, when one sitting next to him turned and remarked to him, 'And what do you think of this Bleeding Lamb?' He was horrified, he said, and started back; he was not accustomed to hear it put in that light. But the words clung to him, and he could get no rest till he himself went and found peace through the atoning blood of the Lamb

"One evening the impression was so great that every one felt it; and he (Weaver) requested the anxious to go out, the men into one room and the women into another. He asked me to go down into the hall, in case some might be there waiting but unwilling to go into the room. Then I learned that eight men were in a room waiting, with no one to speak to them.

"'Will you go, sir?' said one.

"'Certainly,' I answered. The result will speak for itself by the following incident.

"A year after this some one called upon me, and said to me, 'If you want to see John Strachan alive, you would need to come now, for he is dying.'

"'Who is John Strachan?' I asked.

"'Oh, you don't know him; but he knows you.'

"I went to see him, and his first words were, 'Come away, sir; I want to see you once more before I go to Immanuel's Land.'

"'But how do you know me?' I asked.

"He answered, 'Do you remember eight young men who went into a room to be spoken to after one of Richard Weaver's meetings? I was one of them. You came in, and I don't know what you said, but you put your arms around my neck, and I thought it must be a wonderful religion to make a gentleman like you act like that. That night I got no sleep. I knew enough about the way of salvation, and I closed with Christ. I determined then to speak to all my friends of the change which had come over me; and if I had known that I had only one year more to live, I could not have done more, for I spoke to every one of them.'

"I prayed with him, and said I was going away for a few days, but would call again soon. When I went, his landlady told me that shortly after I left he had died triumphantly.

"These are but specimens of the impression produced at all of Richard Weaver's meetings, and of the fruit that remained to the glory of God.

"For the personality of Richard Weaver, I may say that I have had him in my own house, and myself and my family were struck with his refined gentleness. The refining power of the grace of God was eminently exemplified in him. It shone in his face. He was anxious to be able to *study* the Word critically and experimentally, feeling himself to be deficient in theological training. He asked to have a copy of my Commentary on the Gospels, which I was glad to give to him, although his natural insight was uncommonly good."

From Mr. Thomas Wintle, Pontymoile.

"Whatever else is lacking in the national character of the Welsh, it must be admitted that they are an eminently religious people. Whether amongst the dwellers on the mountain sides, or in the glens and vales, in the towns, coal-fields, or other industrial centres—amongst all classes—there is a manifest desire to inquire after that which is spiritual. Many times within the last century the Principality has been favoured by mighty revivals under such Spirit-filled, heaven-sent preachers as Howell Harris, John Elias, Christmas Evans, Dr. Rees, Herber Evans, and other flaming evangelists, till the remotest parts have felt the power, and participated in the times of refreshing from the presence of the Lord.

"This was the soil on which Richard Weaver had to sow the word, which is the seed of the Kingdom, when he visited Cardiff in 1865. Consequently the largest building, and even the Market Hall, were quite inadequate to hold the crowds of people that thronged to hear the 'Converted Collier' tell the story of redeeming love.

"He visited Cardiff several times, with such blessed results that a few friends offered him a tempting salary to remain and settle down permanently in the town. Alderman Richard Cory proposed to give him a fine villa residence in Roath. All these advantages Richard declined, feeling assured that it was the Lord's will that he should continue as he had begun, and preach the Gospel all over the land, wherever an open door presented itself. Swansea, Pontypridd, Rhondda Valley, and many other localities in Wales were visited and revisited, and everywhere the word was with power.

"One Sunday afternoon, when Weaver was conducting a Mission in Swansea, walking down the street he saw a fruiterer's shop partly opened, and several customers standing inside waiting to be served. His quick perception and ready wit led him to go into the shop, and addressing the woman in charge, he said:—

"'Mrs.! I see some one is dead here; you have the shutters up.'

"'No, sir,' said the astonished woman; 'there's no one dead here.'

"'There is!' thundered Richard, 'and the burial will be in hell.'

"Without another word he walked out, and went on to the meeting. The woman became so terrified that she refused to serve the customers, shut up her shop, and followed the evangelist to the Albert Hall. There that afternoon she was converted, and returning home told her husband what had taken place. His reply was a murderous attack upon his wife for closing the shop. The police came on the scene, arrested the husband, and removed the poor woman in an unconscious state to the hospital, where her right leg was amputated. The husband was tried at the assizes, and sentenced to a term of imprisonment. A few months ago, Mr. James Jones, evangelist (one of Richard's spiritual children), was visiting at Bristol, and there saw the one-legged woman bright and happy, rejoicing in that Christ whom she received as her Saviour in the Albert Hall, Swansea, under such remarkable circumstances.

"In 1891 Richard Weaver visited Pontymoile in connection with our Mission. On the first Sunday afternoon, when he got on the platform and saw the crowded congregation of Welsh colliers and iron-workers with their coal-marked faces and horny hands, he was much moved, and at once said: 'Let us pray.' We shall never forget that prayer. He pleaded with God as a collier, for colliers, conversant with all their hardships, dangers, difficulties, and trials; and when, with a voice trembling with emotion, he pathetically asked the Father of the fatherless, and the Husband of the widow, to remember in much mercy the loved ones left behind in that neighbourhood by the one hundred and seventy-six men who had been killed a few weeks before in the Llanerch colliery near by, strong men sobbed aloud, while others, bathed in tears, cried for mercy. Thus commenced what undoubtedly was Weaver's most successful efforts of later years. Probably a people was never found whose ears were more open, or whose hearts were more ready to receive and to be stirred to their depths, by the Gospel of our Lord Jesus Christ.

"He regularly afterwards visited Pontymoile once or twice a year as long as he lived, and each Mission was equally successful. Its influence was felt throughout the valleys of Monmouthshire. Our brother was beloved by all, and became greatly attached to us and deeply interested in our work.

"His last Mission commenced on Sunday Dec. 5, 1895, and night after night for a fortnight Richard preached —though often in much pain—with marvellous power, from such texts as 'The great day of His wrath,' and 'My Spirit shall not always strive with man.' At the closing service he showed evident signs of physical weakness and pain, and frequently afterwards said that he should never preach again—that his work was done; and it is worthy of remembrance that the text of his last sermon was 1 Cor. xv. 57: 'But thanks be unto God which giveth us the victory through our Lord Jesus Christ.' As he warmed to his subject the signs of weakness disappeared; he preached with the old-time energy and fire; and a rich ingathering of souls crowned the conclusion of his public labours in the cause of Christ.

"Richard intended going with us from Pontymoile to Miss Perks' Soldiers' Institute at Winchester, for a short mission; but feeling so ill on Saturday morning he determined to return at once to his home, or what he smilingly described as 'his lodgings in Cheshire,' only to be called so soon to his 'home in the glory.'

"After he reached his lodgings, as he called them, he sent a characteristic letter to our son, and almost from within sight of the pearly gates, one hour before his home-going, he sent us the following telegram: 'Just going home shouting Victory.'"

From Mr. E. H. Kerwin,

the coadjutor of Mr. F. N. Charrington, in the work of the Great Assembly Hall, Mile End.

"We look back many years and recall the stirring, whole-hearted appeals made by Richard Weaver to the large audiences that used to gather in our old temporary hall which stood on the site, before the Great Assembly Hall was erected. Weaver was always fond of the Great Assembly Hall, and whenever he was preaching in or near London, if he had a night off, that night was spent amongst us. The longest time he spent with us was a month's mission he took in July, 1881; prior to that date he had never held more than a week's services. It is with much gratitude that we record thanks to the Lord for the blessing which we received from his preaching. We have those associated with us in the Great Assembly Hall to-day who were brought to the Lord through the preaching of Richard Weaver; and one of those a few days back was relating to Mr. Frank Weaver how his father had been the means of his conversion. This man was casually walking down the road, when he was invited by some one standing outside to come in and hear Richard Weaver. Curiosity led him to accept the invitation, and that night he was converted. Two evenings afterwards he brought his wife, and she was converted. They have both been engaged in our work as voluntary helpers ever since.

"One of the last occasions on which Richard Weaver was seen in the Great Assembly Hall was a memorable one. It was on the Thanksgiving Day, 11th of April, 1894, when the two old veterans, Joshua Poole and Richard Weaver, stood side by side proclaiming the Truth of God to nearly 5,000 Christian people."

From Dr. T. J. Barnardo.

"I gladly comply with the request that I should lay my humble wreath upon the coffin of the inimitable evangelist and veteran warrior for Christ, Richard Weaver.

"My recollections of him date back to the very beginning of my own Christian life. I think that it was in 1863 I first met Richard. He visited Dublin, where I then lived, just as the marvellous revival of religion associated with the ministry of the Rev. J. Denham Smith and of Rev. Dr. Grattan Guinness was subsiding—subsiding, however, only in the emotional character of the work; but breaking out anew on every side in more solid and lasting trophies of divine grace, as seen in the lives and characters of those whom it affected.

"It is no exaggeration to say that Richard took the city by storm. The old Metropolitan Hall, and subsequently the new Merrion Hall (reared in great part through the munificent benevolence of Mr. Henry Bewley) were crowded out to hear the impassioned utterances of the collier evangelist. The influence he exercised extended through every rank : not merely did vast crowds of business people and working folk throng every assembly, but the wealth, fashion, and high birth of the Irish metropolis were also at the feet of the lowly-born pitman. I have seen him in those days drive through the streets of Dublin in the carriage of one of the oldest and most aristocratic families. The wife of the Lord Chancellor sat by his side, and in the seats opposite ladies who were at that time the 'bright particular stars' of the Irish Vice-Regal Court. No man, being what he was, was ever more flattered than Richard without being spoiled : no man ruled more absolutely in his unpolished but gracious way than he did over his votaries.

"I saw Richard and watched him under many circumstances of which little note has perhaps been taken by others. Henry Bewley, the grand Christian despot, whose life, wealth, house, wife, family, all were devoted to the spread of evangelical truth, admired Richard immensely and believed in him. No one, indeed, who came near this remarkable man could doubt his deep sincerity. His unconventionalism shocked not a few : yet it was native to the man, it simply marked his reality. Richard was 'out and out.' His sincerity glistened like a diamond, and it mattered not whether the setting was silver or gold or merely lead, it was the brilliant gem alone which drew all eyes and charmed all imaginations. No reporting could do justice to Richard's unique addresses; and people who had merely read accounts of his meetings might well wonder at the secret of his power. But the whole man was in these appearances of his, and the mere words he used were only one of his means towards an end. I have his voice, his manner, his very theme ringing in my ears, before my eyes, haunting my memory to-day. I can understand, for I myself have felt, why men were thrilled, and why women surrendered themselves to the magic of an oratory that was untutored indeed, but which was touched as by a live coal from off the heavenly altar. I have never heard any one, never expect to hear any one on earth to compare with him in his matchless eloquence. Yet there was nothing that was not strong, manly, in all that Richard said, and did, and sung. And how can one describe these songs of his? No one ever thought, amid the crowds who always filled the building where Richard spoke, of judging his songs by ordinary standards. Such singing was something altogether by itself, unique, standing apart. It was as effective as his speech.

"Richard was pre-eminently a preacher of Christ. Other things might be touched upon, but only as illustrations to let the light in upon his theme, or as avenues that led up to the centre—the metropolis of all his thoughts. He was eminently human too. The touches of tenderness with which at times his addresses were marked, carried one away upon a flood-tide of emotion.

"And I knew him after the great trouble fell like a

dark cloud over his life. I knew him in and through it all, and I loved him—loved him because I believed in him, and as I believe in him to-day.

"Seventeen or eighteen years ago I was in Manchester holding a Mission. There I saw a white-haired, benevolent-looking, elderly man in the midst of my audience, sitting between his wife and daughter. It was Richard. At this time he was conducting the Hollinwood Mission. For years he had laboured unheard of and unnoticed in this lowly ministry among the poor, and many among them had learned to love this wonderful old man with the deep-blue turquoise eyes, whose brightness was yet undimmed by age or sorrow. Out of the talk that followed that little meeting came Richard's decision to enter once more upon the work of an evangelist, to which, indeed, many voices were calling him—voices which he now hoped were speaking in the tones and with the authority of the great Master. I was glad to be able forthwith to invite Richard to East London, and he came. The old Edinburgh Castle was crowded out at his renewed services, for the common people always heard him gladly. Although age and grief and disappointment had dimmed the fire and lowered the vitality of the inimitable Richard, yet the magic of that wonderful voice and the touching homeliness of the Lancashire talk, carried his hearers by common impulse to the feet of Christ. On that first night over one hundred persons professed either to have been led to Christ, or to have been restored from backsliding. That Mission was followed by another. Again and yet again Richard visited us; but at each visit it was manifest the evangelist was becoming less vigorous and less able for the task. Occasionally, however, in spite of all hindrances, there would flash out some revelation of the depths of that heart full of love to Christ and man, and then all would be charmed and held spellbound. I remember too, how at a meeting of workers held at the Assembly Hall in Mile End Road, the old man suddenly arose—Reginald Radcliffe being in the chair—and spoke as only he could speak; and well do I recollect the deep impression made upon all present by his words and looks.

"But I must not extend this necessarily hasty *resumé* of my recollections. The memory of this dear servant of God is green in my heart, and I can never forget the wonders which God did by his agency."

FROM REV. H. MONTGOMERY, M.A., BELFAST.

"I gladly contribute a few words telling of Richard Weaver's later visits to Belfast, and bearing witness to the fact that God graciously used his servant in confirming the faith of his children and in bringing sinners to the Saviour.

"It was the privilege of the writer to stand alongside the veteran evangelist on each of the occasions referred to, the meetings being held in a large circus in a central situation.

"Given that the preacher has the popular gifts, a circus is the kind of building likely to attract the class of people needing the gospel. God had graciously endowed our friend with unique qualifications for reaching and retaining the ear of the crowd. He had a voice of great power and flexibility, a tender heart, a fine command of simple Saxon language, the power of exposing sin and shams of every kind, a mind thoroughly saturated with the word of God, a clear, strong grip of the truth, and an experience in gospel work almost unrivalled. All these gifts and graces were honestly and sincerely laid at the feet of the Master for Him to use as He thought best. With such endowments as these it is hardly necessary to add that large and interested audiences always waited on the ministrations of the evangelist.

"Mr. Weaver was a man who preached from experience. The gospel was no mere theological theory with him. He had been in the depths, and had been drawn up therefrom, and he *knew* the meaning of 'Out of darkness into his marvellous light.' It is said that two priests once approached a French evangelical pastor, and thus addressed him, 'Sire, we wish to enter your religion.' 'Ah,' said the pastor in reply, 'our religion must enter you.' This is how it was with Richard Weaver; what he preached he knew as a personal experience. The experimental in his addresses was what captured the crowd.

"Nansen had a large and ready audience because he could tell of being further north than other explorers. Our evangelist, by declaring what and where he had been, and how God had reached and rescued him, was used by the Lord of the Harvest to attract multitudes to the Cross and rouse large numbers from the sleep of sin.

"Our friend's power of illustration was remarkable. He was never, as far as I can remember, guilty of using an ill-judged metaphor or an infelicitous illustration. In one address he gave in Belfast, on 'Many waters cannot quench love,' two well-remembered historical incidents associated with the Covenanting persecution period in Scotland were most touchingly and suitably introduced—that of the murder of John Brown of

Priesthill, and the drowning of Margaret Wilson and Margaret McLaughlin in the Solway. Weaver had the art of putting truth well, of arranging it suitably and logically. He could, and did, through God's grace, sling *smooth* stones, *i.e.*, present the gospel message in such a way as was most likely, through the power of the Spirit, to effect the conviction and conversion of the sinner.

"I can never forget the extraordinary way in which Weaver on one particular night, when closing his address, shouted out the word '*sinner*.' His voice rang like a clarion all over the immense building, and made almost the very fabric quiver. Even by that one word numbers were roused.

"The gentleness of our dear friend, his geniality, his generosity, made him to live in the hearts of hundreds whom he and we will never know of until the great day. His love for the old gospel, and for bringing sinners to the cross, burned within him a bright flame to the last. He was in feeble health when with us; but the sight of a big congregation kindled in his soul a yearning compassion for the perishing, and drew from him strong crying in prayer for God to save, and save on the spot.

"The circus in which Mr. Weaver preached has passed away; but the fruits of his ministry in this city will abide to the glory of God, and as a proof that the message of mercy is still the power of God unto salvation to every one that believeth."

As Weaver's friend of thirty-five years' standing, Mr. R. C. Morgan, was in Africa, the privilege of laying the wreath of public testimony on the coffin on the day of the burial was accorded to Dr. Barnardo.

He gratefully accepted the honour. Under the impression (got by consulting wrong tables) that the train left London at 10.30, he reached the station at 10.20. To his dismay he discovered that he had made a mistake. The train left at 10.10.

Those in charge of the burial decided to find a man of opportunity among the mourners at the grave. They found the Rev. John Robertson, of the City Temple, Glasgow. He had no time given him to prepare; but he loved Weaver. Out of the abundance of the heart the mouth spake. Thus it came to pass that the outstanding wreath was not a wreath of English roses, but a wreath of Scottish bluebells.

Mr. Robertson's addresses here given are taken from *The Signal* of 22nd April, 1896. In the chapel he said:—

Through Dr. Barnardo missing his train, I am unexpectedly called upon to take this memorial service. Our hearts are stricken to-day. Before us lies the precious dust of one of the most honoured servants of the Lord Jesus Christ of this half-century, honoured by the Master by having had committed to him, more than to any other in our generation, the work of calling sinners to repentance and being made the means of their conversion at the cross of the Crucified. Richard Weaver was a flame kindled by God Himself; and this flame lit up with the atoning love of Christ the hearts of hundreds of thousands of his fellow-sinners. Perhaps it is meet that a Scotsman should have crossed the border to lay a wreath of Scottish bluebells on the coffin of Richard Weaver; for though he belonged to you English people, and loved his native England, his heart nevertheless was peculiarly knit to the "land of the mountain and the flood." It was in Scotland that some of the most marvellous results of Richard Weaver's preaching were seen, and it was in Scotland that the Holy Ghost confirmed the Word with signs following to an extent that thrilled our staid and solemn country into unwonted

"Hallelujahs." Richard Weaver's hymns flew like wildfire on the wings of the wind, and our grave, psalm-singing Covenanters perforce had to open their mouths in the infectious harmony of those new Gospel melodies of his.

GOD WAS WITH HIM, AND HE IS NOW WITH GOD.

The day was heavy in Glasgow when the newspaper paragraph caught our eye, saying, "Richard Weaver is dead." I have lost a dearly-loved friend—so have you. He is not here. The cold frame is not he; his spirit has left it and is with Christ, which is far better; and the precious dust we now commit to the grave, in the sure and certain hope of a glorious resurrection when the morn of morns dawns upon the Church.

I have thought it remarkable, and I think it was designed of God, that Richard Weaver's last sermon in Scotland should have been preached in the very building in which were seen his old triumphs in preaching the Gospel of Christ—the City Hall of Glasgow, where my congregation now gather. Thousands on that occasion thronged round him, and listened to some of the most thrilling utterances that ever fell from mortal lips, commending the love and grace of his Saviour. Will ever any that were present at that last meeting of the veteran revivalist—for revivalist he was to the end—forget his words when he summoned from the spirit land, Abraham and Jacob, David and Isaiah, and all the saints of old, Luther and Calvin, and John Knox, Wesley, Whitefield, M'Cheyne, and Thomas Chalmers, to bear testimony to the sufficiency in life and in death of the grace of the Lord Jesus Christ, and the faithfulness of God! It was the old fervour repeated over again of the great Revival time of 1859 and 1860, and gave some of us that were bairns at that wonderful time a kind of idea of what Richard Weaver and that great Revival were.

God tried him and tested him beyond most, and he stood the test and came forth as gold. His hair as I knew him was driven white; not so much with the snows of age and the coming eternity, as from the blanching of the pain and travail of sadness and sorrow, and I will say, the unmerited neglect and cruelty he passed through. But all is over now; "there is rest for the weary," as he often sang, and he has found it in the bosom of his God. We commend the bereaved widow and family of him who hath gone to God, that He may grant them his own consolation, and as we commit the dust of his servant to the tomb to wait his promise of resurrection, do we not hear the voice say to us all, "Be ye also ready, for ye know not the day, nor the hour, when the Son of Man shall come"? Oh, let us be in earnest, for eternity will soon be upon us, and our opportunity gone.

Mr. Robertson then read 1 Thess. iv. 13–17. Thereafter the coffin was lifted and borne by four colliers who had been converted through Weaver's instrumentality; and was lowered into the grave. A great throng from the city and different parts of the country were present, and Mr. Robertson was asked if he had any further message. Stepping forward, he said:

At this open grave, I have been asked to conclude with a few words. The first time I ever heard of Richard Weaver was long ago in connection with a hymn my mother, now in glory, sang to me.

The traditions of the great Revival of 1859 and 1860, in which Richard Weaver passed through Scotland like a flame of fire, were to Scotch boys like me, as we grew up, like a holy atmosphere. We never saw, but we heard and were glad, and have wistfully longed for that old time of the right hand of the Most High to return. When the annals of the spiritual movements from God on this poor earth of ours are written by the true annalists, the recording angels, one name will be inscribed as a messenger of Christ to our nation, more prominently than earthly historians seem inclined to inscribe it, and that name is "Richard Weaver." Just as Wesley and Whitefield were called by God to call out his people from the darkness and unbelief of a degenerate Christendom, so half-way through this century God called Richard Weaver to summon his people from the surrounding chill and death of formality and indifference. No bishop's hands were on his head—the converted collier needed them not. The Cross was where he stood, and he beckoned sinners to come with their guilt-laden hearts to where he had himself obtained peace and pardon from an offended God. I never thought that he would, in the providence of God, be at my own fireside; that my house would for a time be his home, that he would be loved by my bairnies, listened to by my people, and listened to in his very last sermon in Scotland, in the City Hall.

The evangelical succession is a truth that needs to be restored; and I am surprised to find it too much overlooked in the ordinary survey of those things which led up to the entrenched evangelical position of our churches that resulted from the visit of Messrs. Moody and Sankey from America in the seventies. Pioneers that do the most difficult work are apt to be lost sight of. Perhaps even in this neglect pioneers may be like the first Pioneer of Christianity, the Christ Himself, who came unto his own, but his own received Him not. Let the missing link in the evangelical succession be righteously restored. The link is Richard Weaver. We owe, indeed, under God, the visit of Messrs. Moody and Sankey to him whose body is about for a time to be enclosed in this grave in Manchester. Though strangely it is not mentioned in the published "Life of Henry Moorhouse," yet it is the fact that Henry Moorhouse was converted to God through the instrumentality of Richard Weaver; and it was Henry Moorhouse's teaching and contact with Mr. Moody that sent him over to this country to tell the "old, old story," with such great blessing from God, for which we would praise Him: but in justice let the historical link be realized. Richard Weaver was second to none, and first to many, in natural gifts as an evangelist—apart, of course, from the grace of Christ and the baptism of the Holy Ghost, without which all gifts are vain. The '59 and '60 movement, on which, like a ship on the inrolling wave, he was borne, was weird in its unearthliness; it was from God.

But we will not speak of the servant, but of the Master; we will not mention at this graveside the sinner saved, but the Saviour; we would commend Christ to you all. He has gone home, and we have sung around his grave the hymns that he requested the mourners to sing; and we give God thanks that in his place his two sons here proclaim, as evangelists in speech and in song, the Gospel their father spoke and sang so movingly and long. May God comfort the bereaved! Their translated father told them to put on the tombstone that will be erected on this spot the words,

"A GREAT SINNER SAVED BY GREAT GRACE."

Farewell, soldier of Jesus, fallen asleep! Farewell, Richard Weaver! dear old Greatheart of the evangel. Till the heavens be no more we shall not meet, but then we shall—yes, meet thee, and meet our Lord and Saviour, when we shall be like Him and with Him for ever and ever. Amen.

Here is another wreath from Scotland—a humble wreath of heather sprays, from Weaver's Edinburgh friend and laureate, Mr. R. Meek. Shall I put it in? I don't know. It's badly plaited. But it's tied "wi' the silken band o' love," and that covers a multitude of defects. So I'll risk it.

> And now his sun is set,
>   To rise in brighter day;
> To shine with more effulgent light
>   Above the starry way.
>
> The servant's work is done.
>   O'er many vales of ours
> He sowed the good seed of the word
>   'Neath heaven's refreshing showers.
>
> And into city slums
>   He bore the gospel light,
> Till here and there a ray shot forth
>   From out the darkest night.
>
> Oh, can I e'er forget
>   Those happy, holy days,
> When hand-in-hand with him I walked
>   In heavenly wisdom's ways?
>
> But this is not our rest;
>   God called his Richard home:
> And though I face a lonelier walk,
>   My call will shortly come.

We have heard that sigh before. When? Where? At last we remember. It comes from the "muirland of mist where the martyrs lay." It is Peden's sigh at another Richard's grave. As we think of the rest into which Weaver has entered, we feel that it is natural for a lonely and wearied comrade to give expression to his longings in the sigh:

"OH TAE BE WI' RITCHIE!"

But a far different vision draws our gaze. As we think of Weaver's life, we see a strong man standing by the whelming river of sin. He makes us feel that he dares to believe that the waters of even that Jordan can be divided. He has seen it done, and he believes it can be done again. He lifts on high the old tried and proved mantle: he calls upon the tried and proved Lord, and he smites the waters,

AND THEY ARE DIVIDED.

The signs that followed his preaching were:

"Holier lives,
Tenderer mothers, and worthier wives,
The husband and father whose children fled
And sad wife wept, when his drunken tread
Frightened peace from his roof-tree shade,
And a rock of offence his hearthstone made.
In a strength that was not his own began
To rise from the brute's to the plane of man.
Old friends embraced long held apart
By evil counsel and pride of heart;
And penitence saw through misty tears,
In the bow of hope on its cloud of fears,
The promise of Heaven's eternal years!
The peace of God for the world's annoy,
Beauty for ashes and oil of joy."

How we wish we could close with that vision! But

another keeps thrusting itself in on our unwilling attention. We ourselves stand by the same river. We have the old mantle. As we lift it on high, we carefully explain that we've altered it somewhat. We loudly declare that the Gospel which we preach is "*the old Gospel with a difference.*" The blood-red Cross that used to be the outstanding adornment of the old mantle was an offence to many. So we have removed or hidden it. The mantle that we raise on high is without "the offence of the Cross." In the most approved fashion we smite the waters; but—but—

THEY ARE NOT DIVIDED AS BEFORE.

SOME WORKS BY PHILIP MAURO

THE NUMBER OF MAN
The Climax of Civilization

Strong paper covers, **1s. 6d.**; cloth, **2s.** Oxford India Paper Edition—Paste grain leather, limp, round corners, gilt edges, **6s.** net (post free, 6s. 4d.). [*17th Thousand.*

The writer has set forth some of the results of an examination which he has made of the great social, economic, and religious movements in progress throughout the world. In each one of these movements, he finds indications that the affairs of humanity are approaching *a great world crisis*. Throughout Christendom and Heathendom, Catholicism and Protestantism, Judaism and Mohammedanism, Buddhism and Confucianism, and even Agnosticism, there have suddenly appeared *mysterious forces*, each and all pressing on in the same direction.[1] The author believes that a great world-wide spiritual crisis is at hand, and that two bodies of human beings are now in process of formation—namely, the body of Christ and the body of Anti-Christ. There are few preachers and teachers who may not get much valuable help from this work.[2]

AUTHORITIES:—[1] *Irish Methodist Church Record*; [2] *Christian Advocate.*

THE WORLD AND ITS GOD

New edition, enlarged and extended, with additional chapters. Paper, **6d.**; cloth, **1s.** Special cheap edition, for distribution, **3d.** [*71st Thousand*

LIFE IN THE WORD

Paper, **6d.**; cloth, **1s.** [*22nd Thousand.*

"Freshly written, with a constant and clear recognition of the grave issues at stake to-day in regard to the Bible as the Word of God."—*The Churchman.*

"A fine tonic for any who have been shaken and weakened by recent plausible attacks on the Divine Word."—*Sword and Trowel.*

A colporteur writes: "*Life in the Word* has made many read the Bible afresh. One man told me he thanked God I had sold him this book, as it opened his eyes to see and find life in Christ."

MORGAN & SCOTT LD., 12 Paternoster Buildings, LONDON, E.C.

ALSO BY PHILIP MAURO

MAN'S DAY

Strong paper covers, 1s. 6d.; cloth, 2s. Oxford India Paper Edition—Paste grain leather, limp, round corners, gilt edges, silk marker, 3s. 6d. net (post free, 3s. 10d.)

[19*th Thousand.*

We are here shown the true nature of "Man's Day" — "this darkness," "the present evil age." We see how the forces and principles of "the world"—its gospel and its god—are in conflict with the Truth, and have usurped authority in the Church of Christ. More than that, we see how "Reform" takes the place of regeneration; "Progress" rules out heart piety; and "Evolution" theories dispense with the God and Father of our Lord Jesus Christ, and the gracious revelation given to us in the Holy Scriptures. . . . We find it demonstrated that, however highly educated, the world is nevertheless at enmity against God; also that, however zealous and refined they may be, the works of the flesh are the product of the carnal mind.[1] The title is taken from 1 Cor. iv. 3, where the word "judgment" is literally "day." The characteristics of this age are examined, and an analogy is found between the days of creation and the dispensation ages.[2]

AUTHORITIES:—[1] *The Christian;* [2] *Baptist.*

REASON TO REVELATION

Paper, 6d; cloth, 1s.

A note of special interest applies to this work as being Mr. Mauro's first work as a writer of Christian literature, and penned within two years from his own acceptance of the Bible as the Message of God to man.

"The author seeks to show that reason can never find God unaided, and quotes some of his own written thoughts before his conversion, showing his utter ignorance of the nature of Christianity. He points out how utterly opposed is the teaching of Holy Scripture to the idea that man can gradually improve his own character, and shows that the human intellect can only conduct the soul up to the point where faith can apprehend Christ as the Saviour of the world."—*Rest and Reaping.*

A TESTIMONY, AND OTHER WRITINGS

Cloth, 1s.   CONTENTS.

A TESTIMONY.	THE FOUNDATIONS OF FAITH.
THE PRESENT STATE OF THE CROPS.	THE CHARACTERISTICS OF THE AGE.
MODERN PHILOSOPHY.	ETERNAL RELATIONSHIPS.

MORGAN & SCOTT LD., 12 Paternoster Buildings, LONDON, E.C.

www.ingramcontent.com/pod-product-compliance
Lightning Source LLC
Chambersburg PA
CBHW081324090426

42737CB00017B/3029